Real Love

Real Love

Mary Beth Bonacci

Answers Your Questions
on Dating, Marriage and
the Real Meaning of Sex

IGNATIUS PRESS   SAN FRANCISCO

Cover by Roxanne Mei Lum

© 1996 Mary Beth Bonacci
ISBN 0–89870–613–0
Library of Congress catalogue number 96–76165
Printed in the United States of America ∞

To Lewis Barbato, M.D., who helped me understand human nature; and to the faculty and staff of the St. Ignatius Institute, who gave me the spiritual and educational formation which has made this work possible.

Contents

Acknowledgments 13

Introduction 15

1. Love and Sex: What Is the Connection? 21
   Love 21
   Sex and Marriage 26
   Chastity 38

2. Contraception and Pregnancy 41
   Teen Pregnancy 41
   Abortion 47
   Contraception 56

3. AIDS, STDs and Safe Sex 63
   STDs and AIDS 63
   "Safe Sex" 67

4. Sex and Emotion 73
   Premarital Bonding 73
   Sex in Unmarried Relationships 76
   The First Time 86
   Rape 87
   Should We Get Married? 88
   Guilt 89
   Breaking the Bond 89

5. Chastity, Sex and Marriage 91

Love = Sex? 91
"Ready" for Sex 95
Chastity Is Real Love 97
Living Together 100
Sexual Compatibility 103
Engagement 104
Is Sex Bad or Great? 107
"Choice" 108
One-Night Stands 108
Marriage—Just for Sex? 109
Remarriage 109
Single Adults 109
Never Married—No Sex? 110
Marital Chastity 111
The Church and Contraception 112
Artificial Insemination 116
Divorce and Annulment 118
Homosexuality 121

6. Finding Real Love 131
Not Worthy of Real Love? 131
Finding Mr. or Ms. Right 133
In Love but Miserable? 137
Love or Infatuation? 139
Love at First Sight 140
Does He Love You? 140
Love or Just Sexual Attraction? 141
In Love—But Not with Your Spouse 143
Using 144

7. Healing the Hurt 145
Chastity and Virginity 145

Sin and Forgiveness 147
Starting Over 155
Healing the Hurt 162
Healing the Relationship 166
Can We Be Friends? 167
"I Got Drunk" 171
Unforgiving Friends 174
"He Had Sex with Someone Else" 175
Sex and Your Future Spouse 177
"I Can't Stop" 178
Sexual Addiction 181
Too Late? 185

8. **Walking the Walk** 186
   How Far Is Too Far? 186
   Fantasy, Pornography and Masturbation 196
   Dressing for Chastity 205
   Chastity Guidelines 207
   Occasions of Sin 209
   Sex and Alcohol 210
   Sleeping Together 211
   Dealing with Desire 212
   Saying "No" 218
   Date Rape 222
   Getting Out 223
   College 224
   Sexually Active Friends 226
   Holding out for Good Guys 228

9. **Men and Women** 229
   Emotions 229
   Sexual Peak 234

Teasing 237
"Does He Like Me?" 237
Men Who Respect Sex and the Women Who
    Love Them 238
Men Who Lie about Sex 239
"Why Don't They Treat Us Better?" 240
Women—What Do They Want in a Man? 241

10. **Single Survival** 242
Dating 242
Flirting 246
The "Perfect" Partner 247
"I'll Change Him!" 248
Healthy Relationships 251
Too Busy to Date 254
Opposite-Sex Friends 255
Falling in Love with a Friend 257
Breaking Up 261
Old Love/New Love 269
No Boyfriend/No Love? 270

11. **For Teens Only** 273
Teen Mothers 275
"Going to 'Do It' Anyway" 278
"Too Young" 279
Teens in Love? 280
Interest in Sex 281
Teen Dating? 283
Parents 289
The Media 294
Peer Pressure 295

Epilogue 297

Appendix 1: Sexually Transmitted Diseases 301

Appendix 2: Resources and Telephone Numbers . . . 313

Bibliography 315

Acknowledgments

Thanks to Tony Sbrana for first coining the term "pizza love". This is probably the last time he'll make the mistake of sharing a good idea with me.

Thanks to John Harvey, O.S.F.S., founder of Courage, for his extremely valuable insights and assistance on the homosexuality questions.

Thanks to Pattie Philibosian for taking the time to read and edit yet another of my manuscripts.

Thanks to Tom Booth, for taking my work seriously enough to think about it even while driving, and for consequently coming up with a book title that everyone could agree on.

Thanks to Mike Flach of the *Arlington Catholic Herald*, John Mallon of the *Sooner Catholic* and Peter Droege of the *Denver Catholic Register* for publishing much of this work in column form.

Thanks to all of my family and friends, and particularly my parents, Leo and Lavina Bonacci, for their unflagging support of my work.

Thanks to the parents, educators, administrators and concerned citizens who have brought me to speak in their cities and schools over the past ten years. The organizers work much harder than the speaker, and my work would not be possible without them.

Most important, a personal thanks to the thousands of

teens and single adults who have submitted questions and comments to me. Your input and insights have shaped my work far more than you could ever realize.

Introduction

When I was a senior in college, I attended a lecture series on a subject that, at the time, had not been receiving much attention on college campuses—or anywhere else. That subject was chastity.

Up to that time, I had always been a "nice Catholic girl". I knew the Church forbade premarital sex, and I had complied. I had even become fairly adept at the "I'm not that kind of girl" speech. But I wasn't exactly sure *why*. I knew it had something to do with not getting pregnant and not going to hell. (*You're a nice boy, and I'm sure sex is fun if you say it is. But forever is a very long time, and I don't want to spend it in a climate quite so warm.*) Of course, these aren't bad reasons to abstain, but neither do they give the whole story.

Like every unmarried Christian, I had struggled with questions. How far is too far? How do I know when I am in love? How do I say "no" nicely? When should I break up with someone? *How* should I break up with someone? Why does the Church teach what she does?

Like most people, I found far too few answers.

I had rarely even *heard* the word "chastity". To me, it referred to Sonny and Cher's kid. I was familiar with the term "abstinence", and that was what I was practicing. The problem with abstinence, of course, was that I didn't really see anything positive about it, aside from avoiding the *more* unpleasant realities of teen pregnancy and eternal damnation.

Thus, what I heard my senior year in those chastity talks enthralled me. The word "chastity" brought my understanding of the gift of sexuality to a whole new level. This was not just about avoiding unpleasant consequences. This was a complete "owner's manual" for our bodies. This was about understanding, finding and living *love!*

Human sexuality is a gift—an incredible, beautiful, precious gift from God. I had certainly heard that in vague terms before, but no one had ever brought the reality home to me as did this series of talks. Like any gift, sexuality is designed for use in a certain context—in this case, in the context of a loving marriage. In that context, it is an incredible instrument of the transmission of God's own love and life. Outside of that context, it can be damaged, and it can cause damage. I certainly didn't have to look far to see that kind of damage.

After that talk, I began to look around me and to assess what I had been seeing over the past years. I saw the damage right there in my own generation. But those who were abstaining seemed to be *doing* better—and not just in avoiding pregnancy and disease. Love was going better. Relationships were going better. They were more easily able to leave when things were not working out. There was less turmoil in their lives. They were *happier.*

I had discovered the difference between chastity and mere abstinence. Abstinence is negative. It is about what you don't do. Chastity is positive. It is a virtue. It is about understanding and living real love, not just in dating, but in every area of life.

Real love seeks not just to satisfy itself. In real love, we look out for what is best for the other. That is what chastity helps us to do—to understand the precious gift of sexuality, and to respect it in ourselves and others, so that we can really love each other instead of using each other. That kind of love—real, honest, self-giving love—is rare in this day and age.

At the time I realized all of this, I was working with pregnant teenagers at a pregnancy center. I kept thinking, "If only I had talked to you two months ago." It was so clear to me that their sexual activity was fueled by an unfulfilled desire for real love. I was tired of dealing with the consequences. I wanted to get to the root of the problem.

Then I had another radical idea. "Why don't I go to *schools* and talk about chastity? Others are probably asking all the same questions I've asked. I would have *loved* to have had someone talk to me about all of this when I was a teenager." It seemed like a pretty novel idea at the time. I wasn't aware of anyone else speaking on the subject. (In fact, a handful of others around the country were getting the *same* novel idea at about the same time. Isn't it funny how God works?) Of course, I had no intention of making this kind of work a career. This was just supposed to be the good deed I did on Wednesday afternoons while I climbed the corporate ladder.

I expected audiences to be interested, to be sure. I was convinced then, as I am now, that most people are attracted to chastity, even if they don't know it. I couldn't possibly have predicted, however, the degree of enthusiasm this work would generate. From the beginning, the students gave standing ovations. They kept me after the talks. They asked questions through their lunch breaks and long past school hours. The talks moved from classrooms to auditoriums to stadiums to TV studios; from high schools to college campuses to young adult and parent groups. My first postcollege job quickly went by the wayside, and I dedicated myself to this work on a full-time basis. That was ten years ago, and the work just keeps growing. The harvest is *plenty*. People of *all* ages are starved for this message, starved for guidance and starved for love.

They are also starved for straight answers. One of my favorite parts of any presentation is the question-and-answer period. I always ask audiences to submit anonymous questions in writing, so that they feel free to ask any question without being identified. Over the past ten years, I've been asked a *lot* of questions.

The questions I hear are often wonderful and insightful. Many are very personal. Far too many reflect long unaddressed pain. Many are the same questions I have asked and sometimes still ask. Audiences of all ages, in all areas of the country and in all the other countries I have visited ask the same questions. We all seem to struggle with the same problems and challenges.

I have written this book to answer those questions. Every question you will find in these pages has actually been asked of me. These questions are representative of those I am most frequently asked. Most are taken directly from anonymous questions submitted in the context of a talk. Some are paraphrased from verbal questions asked after a talk. A few are from letters I have received. I have summarized these letters, changing any information that might identify their source, and include them here.

Many of these questions are from teenagers. As a single person well past my teens, however, I know that the answers apply not just to those under twenty, but to anyone who believes it is important to respect God's gift of sexuality while dating.

It is a particular joy for me to work with other single people, knowing that we face the same struggles and challenges. I have always known that those of us who are unmarried need more than exhortations to abstinence. We need concrete help. We need to date well, so that we can marry well. We need to know how to take chastity from the realm of the conceptual to the realm of our everyday lives. We need divine support and, through Him, the support of other single Christians. We need to know that others out there are on the same road we are. This book is my attempt to address those needs.

This work is not mine. It is God's, from end to end. I didn't invent chastity—He did. But I stand in awe of His incredible plan for love, and I enjoy nothing more than sharing it with any audience I can find. It is a blessing and an amazing privilege to be chosen to participate in His work in this way. There is an amazing hunger for love in today's world, and I honestly believe that chastity is the answer—His answer.

Chastity is love—*real* love.

1

Love and Sex: What Is the Connection?

Love

"What are some of the characteristics of love?"

I once heard it said that every person has the same two fears: the fear of not being loved and the fear of not being able to give love. I believe that is true.

It's not wrong to want to be loved. In fact, we were made that way. We all have a desire to interact with others, to share our lives and to join them to other lives. We all want to feel that there are people around us who genuinely care about us and who will be there for us no matter what. That desire springs from our creation in the image and likeness of God. God is love, and as His creatures, we were created for love.

The problem, however, is that it is sometimes difficult to understand what "love" means. People use the word "love" a lot of different ways. Take me, for instance. I am often heard saying that I love my mom and dad. (Those

21

of you who know them understand why I would say this.)
I am also often heard saying that I love pizza.

What am I saying when I say I love my mom and dad?
I'm saying that I care about them. I'm saying that I love
spending time with them and that I talk to them every
chance I get. I'm saying that if they needed me, I would
do everything humanly possible to help them. I'm saying
that I always want what is best for them.

What am I saying when I say I love pizza? Am I saying
that I care deeply about pizza? Am I saying that I have a
relationship with pizza? Am I saying that if a pizza had
a problem, I would be there for the pizza? ("What? Not
enough pepperoni? I'll be right there!")

Of course not. When I say I love pizza, I'm just saying
that I enjoy eating pizza until I don't want any more pizza.
Once I'm tired of the pizza, I don't care what happens to
the rest of it. I'll throw it away. I'll feed it to the dog. I'll
stick it in the back of the refrigerator until it gets all green
and moldy. It doesn't matter to me anymore.

These are two very different definitions of the word
"love".

It gets confusing when people start talking about love
and especially about loving you. Which way do these people love you? Do they want what is best for you, or do
they just want you around because it is good for them,
and they don't really care what happens to you?

Next time someone looks deeply in your eyes and says,
"I love you", look very deeply right back and say, "Would
that be pizza love, or the real thing?"

22

"How do I find real love?"

The Vatican II document *Gaudium et Spes* (Latin for "Joy and Hope") says that "If man is the only creature on earth that God has wanted for its own sake, man can fully discover his true self only in a sincere giving of himself." (GS 24)

Let's look at this quote for a minute. It says, first of all, that God created each and every one of us because, before we even existed, He already loved us. Before you existed, God knew who you were, and He loved you completely for your own sake. He didn't create you because you would "come in handy" when He needed something done. He created you because He loved you, just as He still loves you and wants what is best for you.

The second half of the quote says that man finds himself "only in a sincere giving of himself". Have you ever heard of people who go off to "find themselves"? They generally quit their jobs and go away somewhere, trekking through the Himalayas as if they had somehow "misplaced" themselves in the remote regions of a foreign country.

According to *Gaudium et Spes*, they are way off track. We don't find ourselves through some kind of obsessive, self-centered introspection. We don't find ourselves through going on a vacation or isolating ourselves. We find ourselves through giving ourselves away, through caring about others and wanting what is best for them.

I'm sure you have experienced this "self-discovery" at some point in your life. Maybe you have volunteered at a homeless shelter, a soup kitchen or a crisis pregnancy center. Maybe you have stayed up all night with a sick child or a distraught friend. Regardless of the circumstances, there is a joy and a satisfaction in loving and helping others that far outweighs any inconvenience we may experience in the process.

This is why God created us to live, not alone, but in families and communities. We don't find happiness in living our lives in our own little isolated worlds, spending all of our time and energy just meeting our own needs. We find fulfillment in joining our lives and our needs to those of others and in living lives of loving interdependence, knowing that we are willing to look out for the good of the others and that they in turn are looking out for what is best for us.

Nice system, huh? It's real love—the way it ought to be.

"What does it mean to 'use' someone?"

God created us to live lives of loving interdependence. Because of this "original sin" problem we inherited from Adam and Eve, however, we are not always so good at real love. Instead of looking out for what is best for others, we all have a tendency to want to look out for what is best for ourselves, without caring about the consequences for anyone else.

Using is "pizza love". In using, we treat people the way we would treat a pizza— making them mere "instruments" to satisfy our own desires and not caring what happens to them.

No one wants to be loved with "pizza love". We all want to feel that the people in our lives are there because they care about us—because they honestly and sincerely want what is best for us, and they are willing to be there for us and to stick around when times get tough. It hurts to find out that someone who seemed to love you was only using you.

But how often do you use other people? How often do you date someone, not because you want to explore the possibility of spending your lives together, but because this person is good looking and makes you feel good or makes you more popular? How often do you get friendly with someone, not because you are genuinely interested in this person, but because he has a nice car or a business connection you need? "Pizza love" works both ways. If you want to receive real love, you have to be willing and able to give it. And learning to love—sincerely to want the good of the other—is a lifelong process.

How can you tell whether someone loves you or is using you? Ask yourself one simple question: Is this person genuinely interested in what is best for me? Does this person see me as an image and likeness of God and treat me with dignity and respect?

Love is not just about dating or romance. It is a daily requirement—we need to live it and to give it in *all* of our relationships—with family, with friends and with everyone we meet in our lives. To fail to love is to miss the entire point of living.

"How do I find love, as in 'the love of my life'?"

We will talk about the connection between dating and love later on in the book. But please read the stuff in the middle first. It all goes together.

Sex and Marriage

"I don't understand why sex is so bad, bad, bad before marriage, yet it is sacred in marriage. In general, is sex good or bad? The Church always says things are good or bad only in certain situations and not all the time, which bugs me."

I'll bet a few of you have asked this question yourselves. Actually, I think it would be difficult to be *alive* in this day and age without asking this question. Why does the Catholic Church teach that premarital sex is wrong? There are a lot of voices encouraging sexual activity—and sometimes they are pretty convincing. Why should you listen to the Church?

When I was in high school, I thought that God was just some kind of "cosmic kill-joy" trying to ruin our fun. But as the years went by, I started to look around at my generation and at some of the consequences of the sexual revolution. Suddenly I saw God's plan in a whole new light.

Sex was created by God, which puts it very squarely in the "good" category. Otherwise we'd have to picture God thumping His divine forehead and saying, "What was I thinking? I made sex bad, bad, bad. I sure blew it." God doesn't operate that way. He knew what He was doing. He created the world the way He did for a reason. "God saw everything He had made, and behold, it was very good" (Gen 1:31). That includes sex.

But there is more. Not only is sex good, but it is *amazingly* good, for more reasons than you may think. Why did God create the world? To fill it up with individual, irreplaceable, unrepeatable people—each one of whom He is madly in love with and wants to share eternity with. When He said, "Be fruitful and multiply, fill the earth and subdue it", He wasn't talking about geraniums. He was talking about people. He wanted lots and lots of people, because He is madly in love with every single human being He creates.

How are we supposed to "be fruitful and multiply"? How are all these new people whom God loves supposed to come into the world? This is where sex enters the picture. God needed to design a system to get all of us here. Bear in mind, of course, that God was working from scratch. He could have come up with any system He wanted to bring new life into the world. The stork could have delivered babies. Maybe Federal Express could have done the job. Or perhaps we could have ordered babies over the Internet. Anything could have worked.

But God chose a different system. He designed this system called a "family". In this system a man and a woman love each other so much that they pledge to spend the rest of their lives together. This, if you stop to think about it, is quite a pledge. Have you ever spent a week with your best friend? Did you get along very well by the end of the week? Imagine spending the rest of your *life* with someone—living in the same house, sleeping in the same bed, even going on vacation together. You would have to love somebody a *lot* to make that kind of promise.

When two people get married, they promise to love each other with "real love", not "pizza love". They promise never to use each other but rather to look out for what is best for each other for the rest of their lives. They *give* themselves totally and completely to each other. They give their entire lives to each other.

As they make this pledge before God, something happens to them. God doesn't just transfer their records to the "married" file in the heavenly database. Marriage is a sacrament. Through that sacrament, He actually changes these two people. He joins them together spiritually, binding their souls together so that the "two" really do become "one".

After the wedding, these two people generally go on an expensive trip to a tropical place—otherwise known as a "honeymoon". On that honeymoon, they do something very important. They make love. They give themselves to each other sexually. In doing that, they express with their bodies what they said on the altar. On the altar, they gave their lives to each other. In sexual union, they make that gift real and visible by giving their bodies to each other. In giving their bodies to each other, they give themselves and their lives.

Sex speaks a language, the language of *giving* ourselves to another person. John Paul II says that sex speaks "the language of self-donation". This is the language God built into it, and it is the language the heart hears. It is a language of real love, not "pizza love". It is a language of *permanent* love and commitment, "for better or worse".

So where does new life come from? It comes from that act of love. When a husband and wife come together in sex, God is there, in a very real way, prepared to perform His favorite, most creative act: creating a completely new human being made in His image and likeness. Through sex, the language of love and commitment, new life comes into the world. People come from love!

The end result of all this is a brand-new family. Again, God brings us into the world through families for a reason. He created the family to be the primary way for us to find the fulfillment for which He created us—the fulfillment referred to by the Council fathers in *Gaudium et Spes*. We find ourselves only in a sincere gift of ourselves. In the family, we all give ourselves. No one exists just to have his own needs met but rather to love and to look out for the good of the others, knowing that the others are looking out for what is best for him. Parents earn money, educate the children and sponsor the Cub Scout troop for the sake of their families, not themselves. Children, in doing chores and helping each other, learn to look out for the good of others and to contribute to the larger family unit.

Families are about love. And families come into existence through sex.

So, yeah, I would say that sex is a pretty good thing.

"Couples who are infertile can't create a family. Is their love still fruitful?"

In order for a couple to get married, they need to be able to complete the "marital act". It is that act—self-gift as expressed in sexual intercourse—that defines marriage. If for some reason they are physically unable to have sex, they can't get married.

But a couple who can function sexually need not be able to guarantee that the act will result in conception. Women are fertile only some of the time and for a certain period in their lives. Some women are more fertile than others. Statistically, then, it is certain that some will have more children than others. Some will have fourteen, while others will have zero.

What is important is that a couple perform the act that brings the family into existence, remain open to whatever God wills and then put the results in His hands. He may bless them with children. He may not. If He doesn't, He will make their love fruitful in other ways. The act of marital sexual love between a man and a woman is always fruitful, because it is a reflection of His fruitful love.

"I didn't come into the world because of the love of a husband and wife. In fact, I was adopted, so I don't know what the circumstances of my conception were. If God meant new life to come into the world through love, what does that say about me?"

We need to get one thing very, very straight here. God is madly, madly in love with each and every single human being He creates, regardless of the circumstances of any individual's conception. He doesn't love those who were conceived in marriage any more than He loves those who were conceived outside of marriage. You have value because you were created in His image and likeness, period.

Because God loves you, He wanted you to be born into a family where you could be protected and nurtured. Your parents, however, may have had other ideas. They risked bringing you into the world when they weren't ready for you. But because God can write straight with crooked lines, He still found a family where you could have the love and protection you needed. Regardless of the circumstances of your birth or your childhood, God loves you madly.

Remember, your parents didn't create you. God did.

"If God wants children to be born into families, why does He allow unmarried women to get pregnant?"

In sex, God has given us a tremendous privilege. He allows us to cooperate with Him in the creation of new life. He makes us active participants in His favorite, most creative work.

With every privilege, however, comes responsibility. We can use this privilege well, or we can abuse it. If we risk bringing new life into the world when we're not ready to love and nurture that life, God won't act as some kind of "Divine Birth Control" and keep us from getting pregnant. He treats us like grown-ups. He allows us to use our freedom—for better or for worse.

We will talk more about these issues in Chapter 2.

"Does sex have really complicated emotions with it?"

All of this talk about sex being a beautiful thing and leading to this wonderful family who all love each other is very nice, but we all know that families aren't perfect. Human beings, being tainted by original sin, don't always act in a loving way, even when we are supposed to. And that can be dangerous to marriage and to families.

Think about marriage for a minute. You are promising to spend the rest of your life with someone. That's a long time. My grandparents were married for *sixty-eight years.*

That is an *extremely* long time—and there is a lot of opportunity for someone to get on your nerves.

But God has a lot of reasons to want to help a couple stay together. There is a family to think about. There are children who need to be taken care of. There is the promise they made to be there for each other. But without some help, most marriages probably couldn't even survive petty irritations like dirty laundry on the floor or scratches on the car.

So He built in some help. The same act that creates their family—sexual intercourse—also creates a strong bond between the husband and wife to help them live out their commitment. Psychologists have known for years that sex has an emotional element. Sex is not something you can just "do" with your body and leave your brain at the door. Sexual activity is powerful, and it has profound emotional consequences.

Sex causes a bond to form. I'm sure you're all familiar with the concept of bonding. Mothers bond with babies after birth. Guys experience "male bonding" when they play sports together or sit around complaining about women. Dogs bond with their owners and follow them everywhere.

A bond is a strong emotional attachment with no logical explanation. Babies aren't even capable of being logical, yet they love their mothers. A mother doesn't have much of a logical reason to love this tiny creature who will eat up all of her time, money and energy for the next twenty years. But that bond is eternal and virtually impossible to break.

I recently discovered that, for women, this bond actually has a biological basis. That basis is found in a hormone called oxytocin. Oxytocin is produced by a woman's body in two different situations: sexual arousal and nursing a baby. When her body produces that oxytocin, it works on her brain to create a strong emotional attachment—either to the baby or to her sexual partner.

Oxytocin is the bonding hormone. It is what causes women to feel so strongly attached to their babies and their husbands. Does this mean that sexual activity doesn't cause bonding for men? No. I've talked to too many guys who have experienced a strong emotional bond in sexual activity to believe it doesn't happen to them. We just don't know the chemical basis. (Maybe we should call it "androtocin" or something.)

So why did God create oxytocin? Why is there such a powerful bond in sexual activity? Simple—God knew married people would need some help staying married. Sex, and the emotional bond it creates, "blurs their vision" a little bit so that they don't quite see the petty irritations as clearly. The bond is like the "superglue of the heart", bonding their hearts together so they can weather the minor as well as the major problems of life together. In "giving themselves to each other", they become even more united.

The two really do become one. It's beautiful.

"Does sex have a built-in meaning, or does it just mean whatever we want it to?"

Sex has a meaning. It speaks a language. When we look at everything about sex—the fact that it brings new life into the world, the fact that it causes a strong emotional bond to form, the fact that in giving our bodies to each other we give *ourselves*—we start to realize that God created sex with its own built-in logic, its own language. And that language is *forever.* Sex doesn't just say "I take you for a little while" or "I like your body." Sex says, "I give myself to you forever, and I unite myself to you. I want to join with you and with God in creating, raising and educating children."

Sex speaks the language of forever. It speaks the language of marriage.

"With so many divorces these days, marriage seems to be pretty empty. So why do you have to wait until marriage if you're likely to get a divorce?"

Because people who save sex for marriage are much *less* likely to divorce. Most divorces stem from bad marriage decisions—deciding to marry someone you shouldn't marry. Many of those bad decisions are fueled by the bond that comes from sexual activity. Those who save sex for marriage and spend their single years learning really to love tend to make better marriage decisions and to have much stronger marriages.

I know that many of you are disillusioned with marriage. You've seen so many families fall apart around you that often it is difficult to believe that a marriage *ever* works out. But trust me, it can be better for you. If you concentrate on dating *well,* keep your standards high, save sex for marriage, learn *really* to love and marry someone who can do the same, you will enter marriage with the odds stacked in your favor.

"How can you present your arguments to someone who does not believe the 'ceremony of marriage' is an essential commitment for lifelong partners?"

I'm assuming that this person is not a Christian and doesn't believe that God binds people together in marriage or that sex is a renewal of that spiritual bond. What a shame. This person is missing out on a lot.

You can ask, however, why *not* have the ceremony? If these two people really plan to give themselves to each other, and to spend the rest of their lives together, why refuse to say it in public? Why refuse to sign a marriage certificate? Generally, it is because one or the other *isn't* really sure about staying around forever. If there is no marriage, the back door is always open.

The marriage contract exists to protect the partners. Joining in a lifelong partnership involves risk for both parties. A woman, in particular, takes a financial risk. She often stops working or works at less than full capacity so she can raise children. The marriage contract guarantees that she and her children will be supported. If her husband leaves her, he legally has to give her a significant percentage of everything he earned while they were married. He has to continue to contribute to her support and to that of the children.

If, however, there is no marriage, there is no protection. Either partner can bail out at any time, no questions asked. Why would someone insist on that kind of arrangement?

Makes you wonder, doesn't it?

"Doesn't sex go downhill once a couple gets married?"

This is one of the most common and most ridiculous myths I've ever heard.

In fact, there have been a lot of polls done on sexual activity in America. Everyone loves to do polls about sex. Who's having sex? Who's having sex the most frequently? Who's having the most satisfying sex?

Interestingly enough, they have done several of these polls over the last twenty-five years or so. I don't know why they bother. All the polls reach the same conclusion. The most sexually satisfied people in America, the people who are having the most frequent, most fulfilling sex, are married people. Not just any married people, but *highly religious married people who have saved sex for marriage.*

Why would this be? Is it about technique? Are married people "better" at sex?

Not necessarily. This has nothing to do with technique. It has to do with context. Sex has an inherent meaning. It means "forever". Committed married people *mean* forever. They understand what they are saying in sexual expression, and they are saying it honestly. And they know that the other is saying it honestly. They are truly "giving themselves" in their sexual union.

Married people also have nothing to fear. They don't have to fear pregnancy and single parenthood, because they are committed to staying together. They don't have to fear STDs, because if they are both disease-free and faithful, there are no diseases to transmit. They don't have to fear being used and abandoned, because if they believe in their marriage vows, neither one will abandon the other.

Why do many of the studies mention that married couples who have saved sex for marriage have more satisfying sex lives? Simple. In the first place, people who save sex for marriage are people who understand the meaning of sex. They recognize the level of commitment it signifies and requires, and they abstained during their dating years (which isn't always easy!) out of respect for that language and out of love for a spouse they may not even have known yet. Someone who can do that is someone who has gained a significant degree of self-control, someone who knows what sex says and someone who can be trusted to be faithful. With a partner like that, it is much easier for a spouse to give a complete gift of self, knowing that the other can be trusted with the gift.

Second, a couple who wait for marriage learn about sex together, from each other. They have no one to compare, no memories of other people to hinder their enjoyment of each other. No one likes the thought of being compared to another lover, and for a virgin bride and groom, no comparisons can be made.

[*Note:* I am not saying that people who have made sexual mistakes in the past cannot have a happy, satisfying marital sex life. See Chapter 7, "Healing the Hurt", for tips on starting over after premarital sexual activity.]

"Why should the Catholic Church tell me what to do with my body? It is my body, and I should be able to do whatever I want with it."

I hear this question frequently. First of all, it's not *exactly* your body, is it? It is more like a rental. It was issued to you by Someone, and you will have to return it some day. And, at that point, you will have to explain to Him whatever you have done to it.

Even so, does the Church *make* you do anything with your body? Does the Church have some kind of SWAT team enforcing celibacy on you? (*"We know you're in there sinning. Come out with your hands up. You can't escape—there is a Bishop at every door."*)

The Church is saying something entirely different: God created you, and He knows how you operate. Morality is just an instruction manual for your body. Sex speaks a language—a language of permanent love. You are free to take it out of that context if you choose to, but there will be physical, emotional and spiritual consequences. Abusing that language can hurt you—badly.

Chastity

"What does 'chastity' mean?"

"What is that chased thing you were talking about?"

It's "chaste", not "chased".

When people talk about saving sex for marriage, they generally use one of two words: "abstinence" or "chastity".

I am not a big fan of the word "abstinence" in this context. It doesn't sum up what we want to say. It doesn't even necessarily refer to sex. All Catholics know that, during Lent, Fridays are days of abstinence. Does that mean that Catholics can't engage in sexual activity on those days?

(*"We have to abstain from sex only on Fridays? During Lent? Wow! The Church isn't as strict as I thought!"*) Wrong. In this case, "abstinence" means that we abstain from eating meat.

"Abstinence" is a negative term. It means, quite simply, not doing something. It's tough to get excited about abstinence.

The word "chastity" is different.

Chastity *is* about sex—about understanding and respecting sex. Chastity is about recognizing and respecting the fact that God created sex to speak a language—the language of permanent, committed, married love. Chastity recognizes that respecting that language is the best way to live love.

I also like the word "chastity" because it refers to everyone. "Abstinence" from sexual activity just refers to unmarried people. Those of us who are single don't necessarily like to hear from others that *we* have to abstain but *they* don't.

Chastity isn't just for single people. Chastity is about respecting the language of sexuality, and *everyone* has to do that. I often hear people say, "It's too late for me. I'm married—I don't need to live chastity."

Wrong. Just because someone gets married, he isn't suddenly free to abuse the language of sexuality. Sex is an act of self-giving love directed to another person. Married people need to respect that and to live it. If married sex degenerates into "you are here to satisfy my desires, and I don't care if you have a headache", that person is no longer loving and no longer living chastity.

Chastity is about love, plain and simple. It's about under-

39

standing the role sex plays in love. It's about recognizing that sex speaks the language of *married* love, not "going steady" love or "I am lonely tonight" love. It's about having the strength to respect that language and to walk away from situations where we'd be tempted to compromise it. Chastity is about loving—the *right* way.

In a world with a whole lot of sex and not very much love, I honestly believe that chastity is our only hope.

"How does sex affect an unmarried relationship?"

Good question. I could write a whole book just to answer it.

Hey, I *did* write a whole book to answer it! You're holding it.

Read on.

2

Contraception and Pregnancy

Teen Pregnancy

"How many teenagers get pregnant every year?"

According to the Alan Guttmacher Institute, one of every ten U.S. teenageed girls becomes pregnant every year. That's one million girls.[1] Over fourteen thousand of those girls are under fourteen years old.[2] Of these pregnant teens, roughly four hundred thousand end their pregnancies by abortion.[3]

If the present trends continue, 40 percent of today's fourteen-year-old girls will be pregnant at least once before age twenty.[4]

---

[1] Alan Guttmacher Institute, 1990 report.

[2] National Research Council, *Risking the Future: Adolescent Sexuality, Pregnancy and Childbearing* (Washington, D.C.: National Academy Press, 1987), p. 507.

[3] Source: 1988 data summarized by *Newsweek*, special issue, summer/fall 1990, p. E4.

[4] Claudia Wallis, "Children Having Children", *Time*, December 9, 1985, p. 79.

"Is it possible to get pregnant without 'going all the way'?"

Yes it is. All that is necessary for pregnancy to occur is for sperm to make their way into the cervix. If even a small amount of sperm is deposited outside the vagina when cervical mucus is present, it can make its way up into the cervix and fertilize an egg. So, yes, even someone who is technically a virgin can get pregnant, if she engages in this kind of undressed, intimate contact.

"What if you don't want to get married, but you want a child of your own?"

You don't *want* to get married, but you *want* a child of your own. This is about what *you* want, is it? Let's stop for a minute and think about what a *child* wants. I'm sure that many of you grew up with an absent father. That hurt, didn't it? You saw other kids running around with their dads, playing catch and fishing and going camping. Meanwhile your dad was off in another state with another family, or he was on the other side of town, or maybe he had died. And that hurt.

Children *need* two parents. This is not just a childish desire. We are programmed by God to want and to need two stable parent figures—one male and one female. Many single parents do a great job, but they will be the first to tell you they are doing two people's jobs. It hurts not to have a dad.

But now you want to bring a child into the world, but you don't want to get married. Well, if you have studied any biology at all, I am sure you realize that there *has* to be a dad somewhere. You can't just wish yourself pregnant. So what are you going to do? Have a one-night stand when you are fertile? Speak the language of forever with someone you aren't giving yourself to, or maybe even someone you never expect to see again? Are you going to *use* someone so that you can have a baby for yourself? Will you then refuse to marry this man, depriving him of his child (yes, it is his child, too), because you want a baby "of your own"? Or will you just have yourself artificially inseminated so that you never have to see this guy at all? Either way, this child will go through life deprived of his fundamental right to know and to love his father—watching all the other kids play with their dads while he has never even met his own dad.

This is not about loving a child in the sense of wanting what is best for that child. It is "pizza love", wanting a child the way you want a dog or a new sweater. The child is a possession—something you want in order to fulfill or please yourself, regardless of what is best for the child.

It is best for a child to grow up in a family with two parents and brothers and sisters. Certainly fate intervenes sometimes and makes one of those conditions impossible, but when that happens, the child suffers to some degree. For an adult deliberately to create a situation where that child is deprived of parents and siblings is cruel and wrong.

If a single woman gets pregnant because she made a mistake, then she already has a child, and she has to make the best of that situation. If a single woman runs across a refugee child from Romania who is living on the streets, or if she takes in orphaned nieces or nephews, again she may be offering a child a situation vastly better than the one he came from. But for a single woman deliberately to get pregnant because she wants a child "of her own" is selfish and cruel.

"Please share your view on teenage pregnancy if the couple are in a long-term, committed relationship. How should they handle it?"

Long-term meaning what? The whole semester? The whole year? All of high school?

"Committed" meaning what? Committed not to date anyone else? Committed to getting married "someday"?

There are actually two possible questions here. The first is "Is it okay to plan to have a baby together if we're in a long-term committed relationship?" The answer to that is, "It depends." What kind of long-term committed relationship are we talking about? Dating exclusively? Not okay. Living together? Not okay. Planning to get married someday? Not okay. Married? Go for it.

I am not questioning that these two people may be in love. I believe that teenagers can love each other very deeply. However, they are still young, and they are not yet permanently committed. Until they're married, all of their options remain open. Either one could easily leave at any time. Especially if they are teenagers, they are still changing and maturing and will frequently "outgrow" the relationship. A child is not protected in an arrangement like this. A child is about forever, not "until we break up".

The second question this person could be asking is "What if we make a mistake and get pregnant, but we are in a long-term committed relationship? What should we do?" The implicit question here is "Should we get married?"

There is only one reason to get married: that two mature people honestly love each other, want what is best for each other, want to spend the rest of their lives together and want to raise children together.

This is a very tall order.

Should a couple who weren't planning on marrying, or who are not mature enough to make a good marriage decision, marry just because the girl is pregnant? No. That is just piling one problem on top of another. Teen marriages have a notoriously high divorce rate. An atmosphere full of conflict, discord and unhappiness is not going to help a child. A bad marriage is not necessarily better than no marriage at all.

This is not to say that pregnant, unmarried couples should *never* marry. If a couple was planning to marry anyway, there is nothing wrong with going ahead. If a couple was not planning on marriage, but they are both mature enough to make a good decision and truly believe they are compatible for lifetime partnership, that's fine, too. But I generally recommend that any unmarried couple facing a pregnancy wait until after the baby is born to make any decisions about marriage. Pregnancy is a brief but highly emotional time. An unmarried pregnancy carries with it many profound decisions of its own. It is not a good time to be making other life-altering decisions.

"If you had a daughter and you knew she had a boyfriend five years older than she, and she told you that she was pregnant, how would you react? What would you do?"

Gee, do you suppose this was a hypothetical question?

I am asked at least one question like this in nearly every written question-and-answer session. There are a lot of girls out there who are either afraid they are pregnant or certain they are pregnant and are desperately afraid to tell their parents.

That fear is certainly understandable to a certain extent. If I were a parent, I would not want my teenaged daughter to get pregnant. I would realize that pregnancy would complicate her life and make it more difficult for her to achieve her goals. I would be worried about all the physical, emotional and spiritual risks that sexual activity would pose to her. I would have taught her that sex should be saved for marriage, and I would be disappointed she hadn't listened.

But there is more. Like most parents, I would love her very, very much—more than anyone or anything in the world. If something were wrong in her life, especially something as serious as pregnancy, I would want to know about it. I would not want her seeking help from someone else, someone who doesn't love her and doesn't want to protect her as much as I do. If my daughter were pregnant, she would have a problem. She would need a lot of help. She would need the love and support of her family.

Some teenagers go to enormous lengths, from hiding a pregnancy to seeking abortion, in order to avoid having to tell their parents. I believe this is a terrible mistake. A vast majority of parents, once they get over the initial shock, are there to help and support their pregnant daughters. I have seen teen pregnancies bring families closer together. The best way to turn a bad situation around is to involve the love and support of a family.

If you find out that you are pregnant, my best advice is to swallow your fear and inform your parents. If you are *truly* convinced that you can't go to them, or if your family is so messed up that you fear they would harm you or pressure you into having an abortion, call one of the resource numbers listed in the back of this book for help in dealing with the situation. They will help you determine the best course of action with your parents and will help you to tell them when it becomes necessary.

"My best friend is afraid she might be pregnant. How can I help her?"

If any young woman fears she may be pregnant, she should immediately call one of the numbers in the back of the book. They can lead her to a center in her area where she can receive a free pregnancy test and counseling.

Abortion

"Do you believe in abortion?"

Do I believe that abortion exists? Yes. Do I believe that abortion is good? No.

Abortion can seem very tempting to a woman in trouble. Her problem is the pregnancy. If the pregnancy would go away, her problem would go away. No one would have to know; she wouldn't have to decide what to do with the baby; and she could get on with her life. Right?

Wrong. It doesn't turn out that way. For many women who have abortions, they find that their problems are just beginning. They find themselves reacting emotionally in ways they didn't expect. They often have flashbacks to the abortion experience. They often dream about babies. They often find themselves more prone to promiscuity or substance abuse. Most women who have abortions are in some way haunted by the experience for the rest of their lives. Studies have shown that aborted women frequently suffer from what is known as posttraumatic stress disorder, an emotional syndrome commonly experienced by veterans of the Vietnam War.[5]

Why would women who have had abortions react like a Vietnam vet? Simple. Both have seen violence. Soldiers in the jungle frequently saw violence and death. Land mines and napalm bombs did horrible damage to living human beings right before their eyes. No one can witness something like that and not be permanently affected.

But for women, the violence of abortion happens right in our bodies. From the moment a woman becomes pregnant, she is a mother. A human life is growing inside of her. By the time she finds out that she is pregnant, that life has brain waves, a heartbeat, arms and legs. The

---

[5] Rev. Michael Mannion, *Post Abortion Aftermath* (Kansas City, Mo.: Sheed and Ward, 1995).

new child moves, kicks, wakes and sleeps. He can also feel pain.

What does abortion do? It invades her body. It kills her child.

Now tell me, how does that "solve" women's problems? What problem could a woman possibly have that could be solved by taking her money, invading her body, killing her child and sending her home? No problem I have ever heard of can be solved this way.

Women are not killers. We are nurturers. One of the only true instincts we have is to protect our children. But abortion violates that instinct. It goes against every fiber of a woman's being. It robs her of her role—as mother, as nurturer, as protector.

What kind of society are we that we can't solve our problems without resorting to this kind of violence? A society that respects women? Hardly. A society that protects its weakest members? Clearly not. If we want to move forward as a *civilized* society, we had better find more constructive ways of dealing with our problems.

Women are victimized by abortion. We are not given the facts—about fetal development, about how abortions are performed or about the impact abortion has on our lives.

If you or someone you know has been victimized by abortion, *please* call one of the numbers listed at the back of the book immediately. There can be hope and healing after abortion, and these people can help you find it.

"If you have an abortion and you confess it to the priest, is it forgiven, or is it wrong to kill an unborn child? Do you still go to heaven?"

It is wrong to kill an unborn child—very wrong. Many women realize that this is what has happened only after the abortion has already taken place.

But always remember this: God loves you—no matter what you've done. If you have had an abortion, or done anything else that offends Him, He doesn't love you any less. He still loves you madly. He is there, waiting to forgive you.

If you are sincerely sorry for a sin and you confess it in the confessional, it is forgiven. Never, ever doubt that. There is no sin in the world—including abortion—that He won't forgive if you are sincerely sorry and want to come back to Him.

Take the first step. Go to confession. In doing that, you are going to Christ to express your repentance and to ask Him to set you back on the right path—His path, the path of life. Don't worry about the priest or what he will think. You won't shock him. He will be glad you've come back. If you are more comfortable going to a priest you don't know, or going anonymously, you can do that. Just take that first step.

God is waiting for you. In the midst of all of this pain, He loves you more than you could ever imagine.

"If a woman is pregnant and has an abortion, does her life really go back to just the way it was before?"

No. Her life is never, ever the same.

Abortion has serious emotional consequences. As I said before, abortion takes the life of a woman's child, right there in her own body. That causes serious, long-term emotional trauma. Dr. Vincent Rue, who is an expert in the field of post-abortion trauma, lists twenty-two different studies which show that women suffer profound emotional consequences after having an abortion.[6] Those emotional consequences range from guilt, regret and depression to drug abuse, despair and suicide. Women of all ages who have had abortions suffer from this trauma, but studies show that adolescent women tend to experience severe post-abortion trauma more frequently than their adult counterparts.[7]

For many women, the trauma of the abortion is kept repressed for years—too painful to be dealt with directly. But then something happens to trigger a full-blown traumatic response. Often that event is a subsequent pregnancy. When a pregnant woman sees an ultrasound picture of her very alive, very active nine-week old baby, and realizes that her last baby was aborted at that same age, the reality of the abortion comes back to her full-force. She realizes that it was not a "blob of tissue" that died when she chose abortion, but her living child. And that realization triggers a wave of painful, traumatic grief.

Women who have had abortions are often in tremendous pain. The Christian response is not to condemn but to reach out in love to these women, and to help them through that pain. If you know a woman who has had an

---

[6] Vincent Rue, M.D., in *Post Abortion Aftermath*, Michael Mannion, ed., (Kansas City, Mo.: Sheed and Ward, 1995), pp. 15–17.

[7] Ibid., p. 23.

abortion, please put her in touch with Project Rachel as soon as possible. (The number is at the back of the book.)

Abortions affect not only the women who have them. Husbands, boyfriends, parents, grandparents and siblings are all deeply affected by the "choice" to abort. If you know someone who is suffering from these "second-hand" effects of abortion, Project Rachel offers counseling for them as well.

Don't buy the lie. Abortion does not make a problem "go away". It does tremendous damage—to women, to their children, to their families and to society. It is never a good "choice".

"I've had an abortion and I've confessed it, but I am having a very difficult time forgiving myself. What can I do?"

Please talk to someone, soon. A terrible thing has happened to you. Abortion is a seriously traumatic event for a woman. *Any* woman who has had an abortion needs help to work through the profound emotional consequences she will experience.

Call Project Rachel—the number is at the back of the book. They will be able to hook you up with someone in your area who understands what you are going through and who can help you deal with what has happened.

"Should a person have a baby that was conceived from rape?"

Here is a common question. If a woman is raped, it's not her fault. Why should she have to have a baby, too?

Well, there is one problem. Once she gets pregnant, she already *has* a baby—a baby conceived from rape. The baby is there, moving and growing and developing. And it is not just "the rapist's baby". It is *her* baby, conceived from her egg in her body. So the only question left is: "Should her baby be killed?"

Give the woman a break. She was just raped. She was a victim of a horrible, repugnant act of violence. And now how are we going to help her? Invade her body *again* and commit another horrible, repugnant act of violence? Are we going to kill her child and call it "help"? How is that going to help her? Since when does one act of violence solve another?

I have spoken to several women who have become pregnant as a result of rape. Those who carried the pregnancies to term all tell me that having the baby was a beautiful, healing experience for them. It showed them that God can bring something good out of something painful and tragic. Some kept the babies, and some placed them for adoption. But I have never met one of them who has regretted bringing her baby into the world.

Those who have aborted the babies, on the other hand, tell me a very different story. They tell me the abortion compounded the pain of the rape. They tell me that it took longer to recover from the abortion than from the rape. They tell me that at least the rape was not their fault but that they feel guilty about the abortion because they chose it. Every one of these women I have met regretted having the abortion.

Abortion doesn't make rape go away. It just piles one horrible, violent injustice on top of another.

"Do you feel that a human embryo is worth keeping alive, even if it has a birth defect that will stay with the person for life?"

I am not the best person to answer this question. For the best answer, go to a rehabilitation center. Go to the Special Olympics. Ask a person who was born with a birth defect, "Would you rather be dead? Can I do you a favor and kill you?"

Aborting babies with birth defects is eliminating the problem by killing the victim. Who are we to play God like this? Who are we to say, "Your physical condition doesn't meet our standard, so I am sorry, you'll have to die."

Sometimes people born with "birth defects" are the happiest people of all. But they will never know how happy they can be if we kill them before they have a chance to find out.

"If someone gets a girl pregnant, do you think the couple should use abortion . . . and if not, what should they decide?"

No, I don't think they should "use" abortion.

What should they decide? It all depends on the couple and the situation. Some people decide to keep the baby. A single woman who decides to keep and raise a baby needs to be in a very stable situation—a situation where she knows that the baby's many needs will be met. She needs to be able to stay with the child most of the time or have another very stable, very reliable person who can do that for her. She needs to have adequate financial resources to provide for the baby. She needs to be personally stable and mature enough to care for the baby and to be a good role model.

Most young girls don't feel they are ready for the responsibility of a child. Girls in that situation frequently choose to place the baby for adoption. Adoption, like all the other options a pregnant teen faces, is difficult. But adoption can be an extraordinarily beautiful act of love. Adoption says to a child, "I love you so much that I want what is best for you, and since I can't provide that, I am sending you to a loving family who can."

Modern adoption offers a range of choices, from completely closed adoptions, where the birth mother has no further contact with the child or the family, to open adoptions, where the birth mother receives updates and may even visit the family.

If you asked your friends, you would probably find several who were adopted. And if you asked them what they think of adoption, I'll bet they would say it is a pretty good thing. It gave them the lives and the families they have today.

For more information on adoption, call one of the numbers listed in Appendix 2 at the end of the book.

"Does it hurt your chances of having a baby later on in life if you have an abortion?"

It can. Invading the uterus of a pregnant woman is an abnormal event. It involves forcing the cervix open and often invading the uterus with a knife, curette or other sharp foreign object. If the abortionist slips, there can be holes poked in the uterus. Even if the abortion doesn't directly injure the woman, it can cause uterine scarring or weakened cervical muscles that make it more difficult to carry a subsequent pregnancy to term.

I have met many women whose regret over their abortions is compounded by the fact that they aborted the only children they would ever have.

Contraception

[*Note:* This section is a discussion of the practical aspects of contraception. For a discussion of the moral implications of contraception, see Chapter 5.]

"I am on the Pill. Is that bad for my body?"

The Pill is not terribly healthy for a woman's body. It operates by working on her brain, convincing her that she is pregnant when she is not. By doing that, the logic goes, she won't ovulate, because pregnant women don't ovulate.

However, pregnant women have a whole lot of *other* problems to deal with. They gain weight. Their hormones fluctuate. They get moody. Their skin changes. They get nauseous. They generally don't mind *too* much, because at least they are looking forward to having a baby.

The Pill does all of these things to nonpregnant women. According to Dr. John Rock, one of the original inventors of the Pill, "The Pill has the same side-effects as pregnancy."[8]

---

[8] Dr. John Rock, "The Hand that Rocked the Cradle", *Family Circle*, January 1968, pp. 33, 79–81, 86.

However, there is no baby to look forward to, and the discomfort lasts a lot longer than nine months.

The Pill also has some more serious side effects. It affects the body's blood-clotting ability, leading to significant increases in risk of heart disease and stroke.[9] Women on the Pill are five times more likely to have a stroke than non-Pill users,[10] and three times more likely to have a heart attack.[11] That is hardly what I would call "safe".

"Are Norplant and Depo-Provera safer than the Pill?"

There is no reason to believe they are. Like the Pill, they are hormonal birth-control methods. The only real difference is in the method of delivery.

"What is the failure rate of birth control pills?"

All birth control has what is known as a "failure rate". This means, quite simply, that any birth-control method is guaranteed to fail a certain percentage of the time. I have to admit that I'm not particularly fond of the term "failure" in this case. Birth-control "failure" means a new life —a brand-new person created in the image and likeness of God. That pregnancy may be poorly timed or inconvenient, but "failure" is the wrong word.

---

[9] Bruce Stadel, "Oral Contraceptives and the Occurrence of Disease", in *Contraceptive Steroids: Pharmacology and Safety*, ed. A. T. Gregorie and Richard Blye (New York and London: Plenum Press, 1986), pp. 14–15.

[10] Maureen Gardner, *Facts about Oral Contraceptives*, National Institute of Child Health and Human Development, 1984, p. 8.

[11] Ibid., p. 12.

In a perfect world, studies show that the Pill is fairly effective at preventing pregnancy. However, in the real world, the Pill doesn't "work" quite as well. People forget to take it. The Pill interacts with other medications and loses its effectiveness.

But even when the Pill is "effective", it may not be working in the way we expect. The modern Pill is not very good at suppressing ovulation, so it has a couple of "back-ups". It thickens the cervical mucus, making it difficult for the sperm to get through. And, in case a baby is conceived, the Pill hardens the lining of the uterus so that the baby can't implant, and he dies—an early abortion. According to several experts, these early abortions happen in 2 to 10 percent of menstrual cycles for a woman on the Pill.[12] That means that a woman on the Pill could be conceiving and aborting one baby every year without even knowing it.

"Isn't the Pill an important part of women's rights?"

On the contrary, I think the Pill is very sexist. Women's bodies ovulate every month. That is how we are. That is how we function when we're healthy. That is how we were created by God. Society, however, seems to have decreed that our bodies are not good enough that way. They tell us that, in order to compete in society, our bodies need to be like men's bodies. We can't ovulate. We can't get pregnant. We need to compete on men's terms.

---

[12] John Peel and Malcolm Potts, *Textbook of Contraceptive Practice* (Cambridge, Eng.: Cambridge University Press, 1969), p. 99. See also Bogomir M. Kuhar, Pharm. D., *Infant Homicides*, 2nd ed. (Bardstown, Ken.: Eternal Life Publishers, 1995).

So we ingest a powerful chemical into our perfectly healthy bodies, a chemical that works on our brains every single day, causing side effects like weight gain, mood swings, nausea, blood-clotting problems and heart disease —all to prevent a single little egg from doing its thing once a month.

How are we women supposed to love ourselves? How are we supposed to be at peace with ourselves and with the One who created us if we're living in this constant state of war with our own healthy bodies? I don't think we can. I think a lot of the rage of women today can be tracked to this impossible contradiction between loving ourselves and chemically altering our nature.

The women's magazines tell us that, in order to "compete" in the workplace, we need birth control, abortion and "reproductive freedom".

But we don't. There is another way to be single women with successful careers. We can figure out where babies come from. We can learn how our bodies work and strive to respect them. If we want *real* women's rights, this is the kind of change we need to work for.

"Don't we need to learn about birth control so that there will be fewer abortions?"

Do you remember the statistics I gave at the beginning of the chapter? We have one million pregnant teenagers every year and four hundred thousand teen abortions. There are a total of four thousand abortions performed in this country every *day*, or nearly 1.5 million a year. This is all happening in a world where multiple contraceptive options exist, where sex-education programs spare no detail in describing how those options work and where they can be obtained, where teenaged girls can get any birth-control device they want without their parents' knowledge or consent.

Contrast this situation to the situation forty years ago. There were very few reliable methods of birth control available, and virtually *none* available to teenagers. There were very few sex-education classes, and none that made contraceptives available. Yet there were virtually no abortions and no problem with teen pregnancy in those pre-sexual-revolution times.

What was the difference? Obviously, teenagers were abstaining back then.

It's no accident that contraception and widespread abortion both appeared in American society at the same time. It was expected. Back in 1955, sex researcher Alfred Kinsey said, "At the risk of being repetitious, I would remind the group that we have found the highest frequency of induced abortion in the group which, in general, most frequently used contraceptives."[13]

I'm not saying things were perfect forty years ago, but these facts point to one conclusion—we don't need contraceptives to stop teen pregnancy. We have contraceptives, and they don't seem to be doing the job.

---

[13] Mary S. Calderone, ed., *Abortion in the United States: A Conference Sponsored by the PPFA and the New York Academy of Medicine*, at Arden House (New York: Harper and Row, 1958), p. 157.

"What method is most effective in preventing pregnancy?"

Everyone is always looking for bigger and better ways to prevent pregnancy and stem the teen pregnancy crisis. But I honestly believe there is only one way to prevent teen pregnancy effectively.

That way is chastity.

We need to get back to a more realistic understanding of sex. Sex is, at its most basic level, shooting sperm at eggs. Crude, perhaps, but true.

No matter what we do to try to stop those sperm from getting to that egg, sometimes they manage to slip through. As the old saying goes, "Nature bats last." Fertility is important—it guarantees the survival of the human species. Our bodies, therefore, are very protective of fertility, stubbornly resisting efforts to control it artificially.

"Is it true that at a certain point in a woman's menstruation cycle, she has a lower chance of becoming pregnant?"

"What is Natural Family Planning?"

A woman's body can become pregnant only a few days a month, around the time of ovulation. When she is fertile, there are certain changes in her body. Her temperature rises slightly. The mucus in her cervix changes consistency.

Married couples often learn to interpret these signs and, by abstaining from sexual activity on those days, are able to postpone pregnancy. This is called Natural Family Planning, or NFP. When used correctly, NFP is extremely effective.

Unmarried people sometimes ask why *they* can't be sexually active and use NFP to prevent pregnancy. There are several reasons. First of all, NFP is most effective when practiced in a stable environment with two committed partners. Second, pregnancy is not the only negative consequence of premarital sexual activity. NFP, even if it did prevent pregnancy, could do nothing to prevent AIDS, STDs and the profound emotional and spiritual consequences of sex outside of a committed marriage.

I *do* recommend that unmarried women understand their bodies. Learning to recognize the healthy functioning of the reproductive system and the signs of fertility can help you to appreciate better the amazing gift of your body, and it can help you to recognize when something is wrong—often before the doctor knows.

For more information on NFP, see Chapter 5.

3

AIDS, STDs and Safe Sex

STDs and AIDS

"Why is it harmful to have multiple sexual partners?"

It is harmful to have multiple sexual partners for many, many reasons that we will discuss throughout this book. One of the most obvious, however, is the danger of sexually transmitted diseases (STDs).

Before the sexual revolution, STDs were contracted mostly by prostitutes and sailors in foreign ports. Most of the diseases they contracted were curable by antibiotics, so no one took these diseases very seriously.

Today's situation is very different. STDs have moved from foreign ports into high-school classrooms. Studies show that thirty-three thousand people contract a sexually transmitted disease *every day* in the United States.[1] Many of these diseases are incurable. Some can be fatal. What is worse, these diseases are no longer just for "adults". Ac-

---

[1] Lewis J. Lord, "Sex, with Care", *U.S. News and World Report*, June 2, 1986, pp. 53–57.

cording to one estimate, one in seven American adolescents is currently infected with a sexually transmitted disease.[2] Worse yet, 80 percent of all people infected with a sexually transmitted disease are unaware they are infected.[3]

"What are the most common sexually transmitted diseases?"

Since reading about sexually transmitted diseases is fascinating if you are interested but very boring if you are not, I have placed a complete discussion of sexually transmitted diseases at the back of the book, in Appendix 1. There you will find a discussion of all the major diseases, their nature, course, symptoms, prevalence and treatment.

I will, however, hit a couple of the particularly frightening highlights here:

AIDS: AIDS is the disease that has everyone scared, and with good reason. AIDS is one of the most frightening sexually transmitted diseases ever to plague mankind. AIDS is transmitted through the exchange of body fluid—primarily through blood and semen. AIDS is, as far as we know, 100 percent fatal. A recent White House study reports that one teenager becomes infected with HIV every hour in the United States.[4]

---

[2] Elizabeth Edwardsen, "One in 7 Adolescents Has a Sex-Related Disease", *Cortland Standard*, January 25, 1989, p. 5.

[3] Joe McIlhaney, M.D., *Safe Sex* (Grand Rapids, Mich.: Baker House Books, 1992), p. 23.

[4] Fleming, Patricia S., *Youth and AIDS: An American Agenda*, Office of National AIDS Policy, Letter to President Clinton, March 5, 1996.

Herpes: Herpes is a relatively new disease. There was a lot of talk about herpes in the years just before the emergence of AIDS. Since AIDS, herpes has received much less attention in the national media, but the over twenty million Americans who are infected with the disease certainly haven't forgotten about it.[5]

Herpes is painful and incurable. It causes very painful blisters on very sensitive and private areas of the body. It is extremely contagious, transmitted through sexual contact with an infected person.

Herpes is running rampant in our society. There are at least five hundred thousand new cases reported every year. Currently 30 to 40 percent of all sexually active single Americans are infected with herpes.[6]

Human Papillomavirus (HPV): If it weren't for AIDS, HPV would be very big news.

HPV is a sexually transmitted virus that causes genital warts. That fact alone would be gross enough, but it gets worse. These warts have been shown to be, in many cases, precancerous growths. These growths lead directly to cancers of the reproductive system.[7]

HPV kills. It has been called "the only sexually transmitted disease which commonly kills middle class American heterosexual women".[8] HPV-related cancers kill eight thousand women every year.[9]

---

[5] McIlhaney, *Safe Sex*, p. 100.

[6] Ibid.

[7] Ibid.

[8] Ralph Richart, M.D., "Would HPV Screening Reduce Genital Cancer Deaths?" *OB-GYN News* 24, no. 6 (March 15, 1989): 3.

[9] Ibid.

HPV is also spreading wildly. There are 1.5 million new cases reported every year in the United States.[10] HPV is now the most common reason women visit a gynecologist.[11] One study at the University of California at Berkeley showed that 46 percent of female students tested there were infected with the virus.[12]

Chlamydia: Unlike the previous three diseases, chlamydia is a bacterial infection. Because the bacteria respond to antibiotics, chlamydia is curable. However, since this infection can occur with few or no symptoms, it often goes undetected. Up to 70 percent of women infected with chlamydia are unaware that they are infected.[13]

Chlamydia can do serious, permanent damage to the reproductive system. One episode of chlamydia leaves a woman with a 25 percent chance of being left permanently sterile. Two episodes double that to 50 percent, three to 75 percent, and after four episodes of chlamydia, a woman is virtually certain to be left sterile. A woman can be infected with chlamydia over and over if her infection is treated but her partner's infection is not.

Remember, all of these diseases are *sexually* transmitted. This means that, if you are not sexually active (or shooting heroin with dirty needles or anything like that), you don't need to lie awake wondering if you have an STD. If you *have* been sexually active, I strongly urge you to be tested

---

[10] Ibid.

[11] *OB-GYN News* 28, no. 15 (August 1, 1993): 2 .

[12] H. Bauer, et al., "Genital Human Papillomavirus Infection in Female university Students as Determined by PCR-Based Methods", *Journal of the American Medical Association* 265 (January 1991): 472.

[13] McIlhaney, *Safe Sex*, p. 105.

for these diseases. They can remain undetected for years, and they can do considerable damage in the meantime.

"Can you get AIDS or an STD from oral sex?"

Yes. Engaging in oral sex places a person at very high risk for sexually transmitted diseases.

"Do they have a cure for AIDS?"

Not at this time, and the prospect of a cure in the near future isn't promising.

"Does everyone who gets HIV die of AIDS?"

As far as we know, everyone who becomes infected with the HIV virus dies of AIDS. The only exception is certain babies who are born HIV-positive and then later convert to HIV-negative. This seems to have something to do with being infected by their mothers in utero but having the infection leave their systems after birth.

"Safe Sex"

"How effective are condoms in preventing AIDS?"

I wish more of you would ask this question. Ask your sex-education teachers. Ask your AIDS activists. Ask your local condom distributor. They all seem to be under the impression that using a condom will protect a person from AIDS.

The latest, most reliable study I have seen shows that, in preventing HIV transmission, the condom has a failure rate of 31 percent.[14] And, bear in mind, this is in a controlled setting, with monogamous couples who *know* one partner is infected and are therefore using these condoms *very, very* carefully. I am sure the failure rate for drunk teenagers in a back seat is much higher.

But even if they are using the condom correctly—would you consider a 31 percent failure rate to be "safe"? Would you fly an airline with odds like that? *Sixty-nine percent of our planes land fine—no problem at all. Only 31 percent blow up in midair.* I don't think you would fly with them.

AIDS is nothing to mess with. It kills 100 percent of the time. Trusting a little piece of latex to stand between you and that kind of disaster is foolish.

"How effective are condoms in preventing other STDs?"

There are numerous studies that show that condoms provide very little or no protection against HPV.[15] And, according to the American College of Obstetricians and Gynecologists, "The use of a condom doesn't provide reliable

---

[14] Susan Weller, "A Meta-Analysis of Condom Effectiveness in Reducing Sexually Transmitted HIV", *Social Science and Medicine* 36, no. 12 (1993): pp. 1635–99.

[15] See K. L. Noller, "Talking to the HPV Infected Patient", *Ob-Gyn Clinical Alert*, September 1993, p. 39. See also Robert Reid, M.D., "Condoms Won't Prevent Transmission of Human Papillomavirus", *Family Planning News* 22 (June 1992): 12.

protection against Herpes."[16] There is also at least one study which found no statistically significant differences in Chlamydia infection rates between those who used condoms and those who didn't.[17]

In short, it would be foolish to rely on a condom to prevent the transmission of any of these diseases.

"If condoms don't prevent herpes and some other STDs, how are those diseases transmitted?"

The condom fails at preventing sexually transmitted diseases for several reasons. First of all, latex, like most other substances, is not completely solid. It has microscopic "voids" or holes, that occur as a part of the manufacturing process. These voids can be up to five microns wide. That is too small for the naked eye to see and too small for sperm, at ten microns wide, to pass through.

The AIDS virus, however, is up to 450 times smaller than sperm. That's one-tenth of one micron. The herpes and HPV viruses are similarly small. What does this mean? Simply that these viruses can pass through an intact con-

---

[16] American College of Obstetricians and Gynecologists, "Gynecologic Problems: Genital Herpes" (brochure) December 1985. See also C. Winter, "Counseling the Patient with Genital Herpes", *Herpes Simplex: Diagnosis and Management: Proceedings of a Teleconference* (Morristown, N.J.: Sieber and McIntyre, 1986) pp. 25–27; and H. Wingerson and L. Wingerson, "The Herpes Epidemic: After All the Scare Stories, Some Straight Facts, *Rx Being Well*, March–April 1983, pp. 24–28.

[17] S. Samuels, "Chlamydia: Epidemic among America's Young", December 1989, p. 16.

dom.[18] A condom doesn't need to be broken to fail at preventing disease.

Condoms *can* also fail to protect from herpes and HPV because a condom doesn't cover the entire infected area. Skin to skin contact spreads the disease, and the condom doesn't cover enough skin to be effective.

"Why do you think that wearing a condom is a bad thing?"

I don't think wearing a condom is a bad thing. Go ahead —wear a condom if you'd like. Wear two or three.

Just don't engage in *sex*—with or without a condom. It is very risky—physically, emotionally and spiritually. The condom may offer some physical protection, but not nearly enough to call it "safe". And it offers absolutely no protection from the spiritual and emotional risks we'll discuss in the coming chapters.

Let's get this straight. I am *not* saying, "Go ahead and have sex, but don't bother using a condom." I am saying that the only way to be *really* safe is to abstain from sex until you are married, marry an uninfected partner who will remain faithful to you and remain faithful to that partner.

---

[18] C. M. Roland, "The Barrier Performance of Latex Rubber", *Rubber World* 208, no. 3 (June 1993).

"If someone was 'dead set' on having sex, and there was nothing you could do to change his mind, wouldn't you want someone to give him a condom if it might save his life?"

Let me put it this way. If someone were absolutely "dead set" on killing himself, and there was nothing you could do to change his mind, would you show him the best spot on the bridge to jump from? Or if he were "dead set" on running into traffic, would you give him a helmet?

No, of course not. He's talking about doing something dangerous. You would keep trying to talk him out of it. You wouldn't at some point "give in" and help him to put himself in danger.

Sex outside marriage is similar. If someone is "dead set" on doing it, he's dead set on doing something that puts him at significant physical, emotional and spiritual risk. A condom won't protect him emotionally and spiritually. It *may* protect him physically. But then again, it may not. How would you feel if you gave him that condom, he smiled and thanked you, and then contracted AIDS or HPV despite the condom?

Sex is a beautiful, powerful gift. But used outside of the context it was designed for—marriage—it can be very dangerous, with or without "protection".

"What's the difference between 'doing it' now and 'doing it' when we're married? Either way it seems that you can still get pregnant or AIDS."

Yes and no. Yes, you can still get pregnant. But when you are married, that's not a bad thing. Having children is one of the primary purposes for getting married in the first place, isn't it?

As for AIDS or other STDs—if you are uninfected, you marry an uninfected person, and you are both faithful, you *won't* become infected.[19] That's the beauty of marriage.

"Is it possible for a person to have more than one sexually transmitted disease at a time?"

Yes. It is not only possible, but it is common. Many, many people suffer from multiple sexually transmitted diseases at the same time. Anyone who has sex with them, then, is at risk for *all* the diseases they carry.

"Are there other ways, besides chastity or condoms, to protect yourself?"

No. Remember, however, that condoms may offer *some* protection from *some* diseases, but they are hardly what I would call complete "protection".

Chastity is the only option left. It is gives 100 percent protection—not only physically, but also emotionally and spiritually. It is the only way to go.

---

[19] Provided, of course, you're not shooting heroin with dirty needles or anything like that.

4

Sex and Emotion

Premarital Bonding

"Do you believe that the bond can form without marriage?"

Good question! How often do you see a sex-education class take on this question? Not often. Everyone loves to talk about how sex works, or how to "protect" yourself, but no one ever wants to talk about how sex affects us on the emotional level. As we have discussed, many people seem to think that sex is something that you can just "do" with your body and leave your brain at the door. But that is not true. Sexual activity is powerful, and it has profound emotional consequences.

In the first chapter, we saw that sexual activity causes an emotional bond to form between two people. That bond is an extremely powerful emotional attachment with absolutely no logical explanation. In women, that bond is due in part to a hormone, oxytocin, which her brain produces in sexual activity and in breast feeding. Oxytocin helps produce the mother/child bond. That bond isn't logical, but it is eternal and virtually impossible to break.

Like the mother/child bond, a woman's emotional bond in sexual activity is due in part to oxytocin. And like the mother/child bond, the bond created in sexual activity is very powerful and difficult to break. We also saw that men, too, often bond in sexual activity, although we don't know if there is a chemical basis for that bond.

God created this strong bond in sex for one obvious reason—to help married people stay together. But what happens if you are not married? Can the bond still form?

Yes it can. Your heart has no way of knowing whether or not you are married. It just knows that, in sex, it is supposed to create a bond. So it does.

Some people say, "Well, I would just be very strong and logical, and I would not allow the bond to form." I usually respond, "Good idea! And while you're at it, think very very hard, and *make your blood run backward.*" This bond isn't something you can consciously control. It happens deep down within your psyche. You may not even be consciously aware of it. Whether you are aware of it or not, however, the bond formed in sexual activity is extremely, extremely powerful.

"How come men don't become so emotionally attached to women they have sex with?"

Oxytocin causes women to feel strongly attached to their babies and their husbands. Does this mean that sexual activity doesn't cause bonding for men?

I don't believe it. As I stated in Chapter 1, I have talked to too many guys who have experienced this—guys who have been *devastated* at the breakup of a sexual relationship or a marriage—not to believe that males bond emotionally in sexual activity. The bond may not be as strong as it is in females. It may operate more on the subconscious level. But I'm certain that it is there.

We will talk more about men and emotion in the upcoming sections.

"Can the bond form if you haven't 'gone all the way'?"

Yes. Bonding does occur in sexual activity that stops short of intercourse. That bond can be strong, although probably not as strong as the bond that results from sexual intercourse. It is there nonetheless, and it is strong enough to mess up a dating relationship *badly*.

The very *beginnings* of bonding can come even earlier. Most single people have, at one point or another, started dating someone and thought immediately, "This is not the right one." Then, after that first passionate kiss, they say to themselves, "Well, maybe this could work out after all." Six months later they are still in relationships that don't work, and they realize they had been right in the first place.

Sex in Unmarried Relationships

"How does the bond affect unmarried people?"

Allowing a sexual bond to form can really mess up your dating life.

What is the purpose of dating, anyway? Is it to find the best-looking girlfriend so that you look good in a restaurant? Is to find a guy with a hot car so you don't have to take the bus?

No and no. Dating, plain and simple, is about finding out if you want to get married, and if so, to whom. It is about finding out what kind of person you are compatible with, so that you can make a good marriage decision. It is about getting to know another person very, very well, so that you can figure out if you want to give him or her your life and your children.

In order to do all that, what do you need? You need freedom to come and go. You need to be able to *stop* dating someone if you decide you are not compatible.

Imagine that you are dating someone. At first you really like this person, and everything is terrific. Then, as time goes on, you find out that (a) this person gets on your nerves; (b) this person is also dating your best friend; (c) this person is a drug dealer; or (d) all of the above. You need to *dump this person*. Fast.

What happens, however, if there has been a sexual relationship? What happens if this "superglue of the heart" has formed? Your vision is blurred. You are not seeing clearly.

You have given yourself completely, and that makes it much more difficult to acknowledge that this relationship may not work out.

At this point, many single people utter the universal Christian single person cry: *"I'll change him!"* (or *"her!"*, if you are male). "Yes", you decide. "I'll change him. Sure he's a drug dealer with a felony-conviction record as long as my arm, but I'll change him. Under my care, he will become a rosary-reciting, Mass-attending pillar of the community. He'll change because he loves me."

Some people go a different route—the route of denial. "Sure he deals drugs, but he wouldn't do it in front of the children." Or, "I know she's promiscuous, but she wouldn't cheat on *me.*"

This, as you may have guessed, is not good. This kind of premature bonding does not lead to happy, productive lives. It leads to pain and misery.

Allowing the bond to form can lead to poor marriage decisions. Once a bond forms, the brain is no longer in charge. Feelings take over, drowning out logic. And in making a decision as important as choosing a life partner, you need all the logic you can get.

Marriage decisions are difficult even *without* the bond. Ask people how you will know when you are in love, and they will probably answer, "Oh, you'll know in your heart." Wrong. Your heart is only half of the equation. Your head is the other part, and it plays a very important role. Your brain has to ask the tough questions: Who is this person? Will this person make a good partner? Does this person share my faith? Does this person have sexual self-control? (Do you want to marry a person with no sexual self-control? I don't, because I watch *The Young and the Restless.* I know what's out there.)

The heart doesn't always want to hear the answers to these questions. But they have to be asked, and answered, honestly. The rest of your life is at stake.

Once there has been sexual activity and the bond has formed, however, these questions are even more difficult to answer honestly. The heart has a vested interest in keeping the relationship together. It becomes easier and easier to rationalize. We want to close our eyes to the reality of the situation because ending the relationship would mean breaking the bond, and that thought is too painful to contemplate. So we often choose to ignore the negatives and hope for the best.

"I love my boyfriend very much. We are considering having sex. How will it affect me and our relationship?"

"Does premarital sex strengthen a relationship or hurt it? Why?"

A lot of people *like* the idea of a bond forming in their relationship. They say, "Ooh, cool, a bond. That is *exactly* what we need. We *know* we're getting married. But first we have to take jobs in separate states, or go to separate colleges, or finish graduate school, or make a million dollars. But if we have sex, the bond will keep our love alive. Then when we have our BMWs and our MBAs, we will get married and have a white picket fence and 1.2 children, and the bond will have saved the day."

Does it work that way?

No.

As logical as all of this seems, there is one problem. Sex speaks the language of "I give myself to you totally and completely *now*. I have already committed my life to you. We *are* married, and with this act I renew that sacrament."

Unmarried relationships, by definition, don't speak this language. A "committed" unmarried relationship means basically that "I promise not to date anyone else until I dump you." That is not a real commitment. It is a temporary commitment, and nothing about the language of sex is temporary.

So what happens when sexual activity enters into an unmarried relationship? The body is saying "I give myself totally and completely to you and to what's best for you for the rest of my life." And the heart is hearing that message loud and clear. Meanwhile, the *relationship* is saying something different. It may be saying, "*Hopefully* we will get married." Or maybe "We'll see what happens." Or my personal favorite, "But we're still free to do this with *other* people, right?" Either way, you are not married, and your heart is placed in a very difficult situation.

Sex puts pressure on unmarried relationships. Deep down, your heart knows that it has given itself completely. The relationship, however, isn't at a level of commitment where that gift can be protected. You have given yourself completely, and you know that, as a result, you could be rejected completely. That realization leads to a tremendous amount of vulnerability, insecurity and fear.

Those of us who work with teens or young adults can often tell when a couple first begins to have sex. They don't suddenly have a wonderful, dreamy relationship. Instead, they often begin to fight. She is always crying; he is always mad. They don't necessarily break up, because with the new bond they've formed, they feel attached to each other. But there is a new pressure on the relationship —a pressure they don't understand but that they can't escape.

The other sign that a couple is sexually active is that normally secure women often become very clingy and insecure, and many normally reasonable men suddenly become extremely jealous and possessive. Often they don't even understand why they are behaving this way. But they find it very difficult to stop. That isn't surprising. They have given themselves completely, but they are not in a relationship where that gift can be protected. They suddenly feel extremely vulnerable. That vulnerability puts pressure on them and on their relationship.

Once the gift of self has been given in sexual activity, it becomes easy to lose perspective. The most important consideration is no longer, "Is this the best person for me?" It becomes instead, "This person *can't* reject me." The prospect of giving self and being rejected is so terrifying that we forget to ask if the relationship is even worth keeping.

In all my years in chastity education and my entire life as a single person, I have never seen an unmarried relationship improve as a result of sexual activity. This is very important, so I repeat: *I have never seen an unmarried relationship improve as a result of sexual activity.* I have seen sexual activity hurt relationships. I have seen good relationships fall apart after the onset of sexual activity. I have seen a lot of people *try* to use sex to improve their relationships. But I have never seen it work.

I know that sexual activity can be extremely tempting in an unmarried relationship. When two people love each other, as single people of all ages often do, it is natural to want to express that love physically. Likewise, when a relationship starts to slip away, the temptation to try to "glue" it back together with sex can become almost overwhelming.

But it doesn't work. It doesn't help. Sex speaks one language and one language alone. And that language is, "You and I, now and forever, sacramentally united, ready for whatever happens." It means marriage, and marriage alone. Out of that context, sex can mess up a relationship—badly.

"When a man and a woman love each other and they have sex, why is it different between them after it has happened?"

What a perceptive question! It is true—it *is* different between two people after they have sex. Sex changes them, and their relationship, forever.

There is a reason for that—things are *supposed* to be different. Sex is supposed to bond two people together for life. It is supposed to be the ultimate expression of physical intimacy, reflecting a relationship that has achieved a high degree of emotional and spiritual intimacy. Most importantly, it is supposed to reflect a gift—not a loan—of self to the other.

When a couple isn't married, the relationship change brought about by sex is often a change for the worse. They have spoken a language—that incredibly intimate language of "I give myself to you, and only you, forever." But often they know, consciously or subconsciously, that they have not spoken it with complete honesty. They know that their relationship is not certain to be permanent. They know that their emotional and spiritual intimacy is not as complete as their physical expression would indicate. They know that, to one extent or another, they have spoken this language dishonestly.

That realization, whether conscious or unconscious, can make them profoundly uncomfortable. Anything "temporary" about their relationship can suddenly come into magnified focus. Slights and hurts can become magnified. The way they view each other and the relationship can become distorted. There is often tremendous pressure on the relationship.

Once this pressure appears, a vicious circle begins. A couple will often keep going back to sexual activity, trying to recapture the closeness and intimacy they fear they have lost. Eventually, the relationship can begin to revolve around sex, with emotional intimacy dropping off and larger issues left unresolved.

No, things are never quite the same again.

"When a man and a woman fall in love and have sex, will the relationship most likely break up?"

It is impossible to say that if a couple has sex, they definitely will or will not break up. Each case is unique.

Maybe these two people really love each other. But if they try to express that love through sexual expression, they are putting their relationship at risk in many ways. First of all, they are putting *each other* at risk—emotionally, physically and spiritually. Second, they are risking "blurring their vision" and making a poor marital decision. That is not loving behavior.

If a couple has sex, there are three possible outcomes. The pressure sex puts on a relationship may cause their relationship to break up—whether or not it could have been a good relationship. The bond sex forms could also lead them to marry even if marriage would not be a good decision for them.

The third possible outcome is that the couple may marry and live happily ever after. This, unfortunately, is the least likely outcome. First of all, the percentage of people who actually marry their high-school sweethearts is rather small. Among those who marry in their teens, the divorce rate is extremely high.

There may be couples who had sex in high school and went on to live "happily ever after". But they are the minority, and the *extremely* lucky ones. Most couples who play the odds aren't so lucky.

"Does the bond always form?"

"Do you think it's possible not to have an emotional bond with someone you have had sex with? It seems possible because there are so many people who are always with different partners yet never really care for them."

Nearly every high-school, college and singles' group has a certain percentage of people we would call "loose" or "promiscuous", or other words I won't print. The rest of us tend to look down our noses at people like that, feeling morally superior to them because we have not committed their particular brand of sin.

What is the deal with these people? How are they able to have sex so frequently and with so many different people without seeming to experience that powerful "superglue of the heart" we have been discussing—the emotional bond of sexual activity?

When a person loses his or her virginity, a strong bond always tends to form. But then, often, the relationship breaks up. The bond is broken. "Love" is gone. Different people react in different ways. Some recognize that sex isn't the place to look for love, and they turn to God, friends or family to provide them with the love they need.

Others, especially the particularly needy ones, often take a different approach. They go looking for love, again, in sex. It is the only way they know. Eventually *that* relationship breaks up too, the bond has broken again, and they are back in the cycle. But something begins to happen. They know they've been hurt before, and they don't want to be hurt again. So they "harden their hearts" a little bit. They become distrustful and protective. They still give their bodies, but they try not to give themselves. Each time the bond breaks, their hearts become a little more "scarred". Eventually, they lose the ability to bond altogether.

Think of a piece of duct tape. If you stuck it to your arm and then tore it off, it would hurt. But if you stuck that same piece to your arm again and tore it off again, it wouldn't hurt so much. Some of the "stick' would be gone. If you kept going, eventually the tape would not stick at all.

This is what can happen to people when they become promiscuous. Their hearts lose their adhesiveness, their ability to bond in sexual activity. People like this often say they don't care about love, that they don't believe it exists or that sex for them is just for "fun". Their compulsive sexual activity, however, is still fueled by their need for real love, even if that need has become so repressed that they are no longer consciously aware of it.

The loss of the ability to bond is particularly damaging when this person gets married. That bond is helpful in marriage. It is a necessity, if a marriage is going to weather all the challenges it faces. But a person who can no longer bond won't have that help, even in marriage. The marital sexual relationship will be handicapped from the start. Without the unity that comes from healthy marital sexual intimacy, a couple is almost always bound for trouble.

Does this mean there is no hope for people whose promiscuity has caused them to lose their ability to bond? Of course not. As always, the hope comes through reconciliation in Christ. Anyone who sincerely repents, who begins to live a life of chastity and who learns to turn to God, friends and family to meet his love needs, will find an eventual reestablishment of his ability to bond. It may not be easy or immediate, but it will happen.

I once talked to a man who was feeling guilty about a sexual encounter he'd had with a woman he wasn't dating. I mentioned that what he had done was damaging to her, and he said, "It doesn't matter to her. She's just a slut."

Wrong. It does matter. On the outside, you may see a cold, hard, insensitive person. But I guarantee that, on the inside, there is pain and a love need trying desperately to be met.

From now on, try to look a little bit differently at the "sluts"—the promiscuous people you run into at singles' spots or school or wherever. They are not necessarily evil. It is more likely that they are lonely, and they are trying to cure that loneliness in a way that will never, ever work.

The First Time

"Why do you have a hard time getting away from the first person you've had sex with?"

First sexual experiences tend to leave particularly strong impressions and to create a powerful bond. In fact, among women, many psychologists have found a phenomenon called "imprinting". According to them, when a woman has sex for the first time, the image of her partner becomes "imprinted" on her mind—in an extremely strong and permanent way.

I have no doubt that imprinting happens. I have seen it. I have seen happily married women who don't understand why they still "can't get over" a boyfriend they have not seen in decades. I have seen normally stable women completely "freak out" when the person to whom they lost their virginity gets married.

God created this process for a reason. Sex is for marriage. If a woman saves sex for marriage, then this imprinting will happen with her husband. *He* will be the one she feels permanently attached to. His will be the imprint that stays in her mind, and the resulting bond will serve to strengthen the marriage.

Women experiencing the effects of premarital imprinting are often frightened or upset by what is happening to them. They don't understand how they could remain obsessed by someone who wasn't even necessarily good for them. They often tell me they think they are going crazy. But they are not. Imprinting is normal. What isn't normal is to allow imprinting to happen with someone who isn't going to stick around forever.

Rape

"What about someone who has been raped? Will that person form a bond with the rapist?"

No. Bonding is tied primarily to sexual arousal, which isn't present in the case of someone being forced to have sex against her will. Someone being raped or sexually abused will not bond with her attacker.

Rape cannot be equated with sex any more than breaking and entering can be equated with hospitality. Rape is not just a sexual act. It is a horrible, violent, invasive crime.

Someone whose only experience with sex has been being raped or molested is, in the eyes of God, a virgin. Virginity has to be *given* away. It can't be violently taken.

If you or someone you know has been a victim of rape, molestation or incest, *get help immediately*. Tell someone you trust—your parents, a priest, a church youth leader, a good Christian therapist, anyone. If there is no one to talk to, call one of the numbers in the back of this book. These crimes cause significant trauma, and their victims need immediate help. Without counseling, rape and incest victims often become involved in promiscuous sexual activity in an (unsuccessful) effort to distance themselves from the rape. The success of a future marriage can be threatened by unresolved issues related to the rape.

Rape and incest are horrible crimes, and they leave their victims terribly scarred. With the love of Christ and the help of a professional, Christian therapist, those scars can be faced and healed. Those victims need that help as soon as possible.

Should We Get Married?

"If an unmarried couple has sex, should they get married because they have spoken the 'language of marriage'?"

No, no, a thousand times no. We will discuss marriage more throughout the book. For now, suffice it to say that there is only one reason to get married—you have found the person you want to spend the rest of your life with and you trust enough to give your children to.

Sure, it is difficult to leave someone behind after that bond has formed. That pain, however, is nothing compared to the pain of making a bad marriage decision. Marriage is for keeps. Don't decide lightly.

Guilt

"Why do some people feel guilty after they've been with a guy?"

Guilt can be a good thing. It is our mind's way of telling us, "Something is wrong here." When you're feeling guilty, don't just try to make the guilty *feeling* go away. The best thing to do is to figure out where that feeling came from and what it is telling you. Then deal with the *situation*.

Something very deep inside each of us tells us that sex is about forever and that it is not something to take lightly. People who try to ignore or bury that little voice are making a big mistake. It is much smarter to listen to it.

Breaking the Bond

"What do you do when the bond has formed, you've been together for years, and now you know that he isn't right for you, but every time you break up, both of you go right back together again?"

"I just got out of a relationship where I was sleeping with the guy. We broke up, but I can't get him out of my mind. Will that bond ever go away?"

These kinds of questions are so important that I dedicated a whole chapter to them later in the book. I wanted to mention them here, however, so that you wouldn't think that I would ignore such important issues. We will discuss them soon.

5

Chastity, Sex and Marriage

Love = Sex?

"If I love my girlfriend, why can't I make love to her?"

Finally, the big question. If sex is "making love", and I love someone, why can't I express that love by making love? Seems simple, doesn't it?

First of all, I want to make it clear that I do believe the couple involved may be in love—truly, deeply in love. But is sex outside of marriage a good *expression* of love? That is a different question.

What is love? Remember what we discussed? Love, *real* love, is above all about wanting what is best for the other person. It is about caring about that person's well-being. Love means never, ever unnecessarily putting that person at any kind of risk.

Well, what have we been talking about for the last three chapters? We have been talking about risks—all kinds of significant, serious risks involved in sex outside of marriage.

91

Premarital sex is dangerous physically. It leads to the spread of sexually transmitted diseases, many of which are life-changing or even fatal. Sex is also the number one cause of pregnancy in this country. Pregnancy isn't a disease, but we have talked about how it isn't a good situation for an unmarried woman who isn't equipped to raise and care for a child.

Is it loving a single woman to put her at risk of pregnancy? Is it loving to put someone at risk of sexually transmitted diseases? In sexual activity, that is what is happening, regardless of how you may try to "protect" each other.

There is also a deeper level of risk in sexual activity. In sex, your body is speaking a language. Sex says, "forever, committed, permanent, exclusive", and that is what the heart hears. But in an unmarried relationship, you don't have that level of commitment. You are speaking the language of the body in a lie. You are allowing that bond to form when your relationship can't back it up. That is *not* looking out for the welfare of the other person.

If you "love" your girlfriend, you want what is best for her. You don't want any of these things to happen to her. You want to her have a rich, full life and to reach her fullest potential. You want to protect her, physically and emotionally.

"Making love" to her is not the way to do that.

"I want to have sex with my boyfriend because it's the only way I can show him how much I love him."

Many single people feel this way. They honestly love each other, they honestly want what is best for each other, and they want to express their love sexually.

I am not questioning their love for each other. Maybe their love is real and sincere. If, however, they are trying to express that love sexually outside of marriage, they are not thinking about what they are doing. What does sex prove? Does it prove that they are looking out for each other? Does it prove that they would sacrifice for each other? No. All that sex *proves* is that they are willing to use their bodies to lie to each other, and to put each other at risk, just to make each other "feel good" for a while. That is not an expression of love.

If you really want to prove that you love him, do something good for him, something totally unselfish. Bake him cookies. Sneak over to his house and wash his car. Do something that costs you something—in money or time or effort.

I met a man once who told me that when he was engaged to his wife, he sneaked over to her house one night while she slept. Her parents let him in. He went to her room, and quietly slipped eighty helium balloons through the door, one by one. Each had a note attached, describing the different reasons why he loved her.

That is an act of love.

"My girlfriend says that if I really loved her, I'd prove it by having sex with her."

When someone pressures you for sex, does this person love you? Is she (or he—it works both ways) looking out for what is best for you? In this case, she is asking you to put yourself at risk, to allow yourself to be used—and to force you to put her at risk and use her, so that you can both feel good for a few minutes.

Don't fall for pressure like that. Anyone who pressures you for sex isn't loving you. If someone won't take "no" for an answer, there is one thing left to say. "Good-bye." I am serious. Do *not* hang around in a relationship where you are being pressured for sex. You are with someone who doesn't love you and doesn't want what is best for you.

Compare this person with someone who says, "I am very attracted to you, but I know sex isn't what is best for you or for our relationship. So even though I physically *want* to have sex with you, I won't." *That* is someone who loves you and is able to put your good above her own selfish interest.

Don't waste your time with people who want to use you. Hold out for real love, no matter how long it takes. I assure you, it is worth it.

"I am not Catholic. I am not even a Christian.
I don't want to have sex, but I need a good
excuse for all my friends who are pressuring
me to. What do I say?"

Premarital sex is wrong, plain and simple, because it is not
a loving thing to do. In sexual activity, you put yourself and
another person at risk. There are physical and emotional
consequences, and those consequences exist whether you
believe in God or not.

"Ready" for Sex

"How do I know when I am ready?"

"How do you know if a girl is ready for sex?"

If I had a quarter for every time I have been asked this
question, I would be a very rich woman.

It is no wonder this is a common question. This idea
of being "ready" for sex is everywhere. Sex-education programs encourage students to wait until they are "ready".
Every single television show with a female teenaged cast
member has had at least one episode where the girl is being
pressured for sex but decides not to because she "doesn't
feel ready".

Do you ever wonder about these girls? How do they
know? What determines whether or not they are ready
for sex? Is there some kind of alarm that suddenly goes
off in their heads? Is this some version of the biological

clock? And what good does it do them to be ready? Does being "ready" make sex any different? Does it make sex any better? Does it protect them from anything?

I debated a sexologist on a TV show once.[1] She said that sex is okay for teenagers when they've encountered their "sensation of readiness", which she likened to "the feeling you get when you can dive off the diving board and not climb back down the ladder".

How helpful.

The problem with her approach, and with the whole "ready" concept, is that it relies strictly on feelings. Feelings can change rather frequently. (In my case, every 4.5 seconds or so.) Feelings are inside of us, unlike consequences, which are outside of us. Consequences don't care how we "feel". They happen anyway. Feelings alone, therefore, are not very helpful in making important decisions.

For instance, if you are trying to decide whether to dive off a diving board, would the most important question be how ready you *feel*? Maybe you feel very ready. Maybe you have visualized the perfect dive. Maybe your form is perfect, and your bathing suit looks great. You feel ready.

But there is no water in the pool.

Will "feeling ready" help you? No. You are going die as soon as you hit the bottom, and it doesn't matter how ready you "felt". Feelings are inside of you, but the pool is on the outside, and it doesn't care how you feel.

Sex works the same way. When someone goes to the doctor with a sexually transmitted disease, the doctor never says, "You had a sexual relationship before you felt ready,

---

[1] Yes, she really was a sexologist. She had her Ph.D. in sexology. Don't ask.

didn't you? If you had felt ready, this never would have happened."

Sexual activity carries very real consequences. "Feeling ready" won't protect you from any of them.

Being *really* ready for sex means understanding all of the consequences—physical, emotional and spiritual. Being ready means being in a situation where you don't have to fear any consequences. It means being with one permanently faithful partner who won't leave you and won't infect you. It means being in a situation where pregnancy doesn't have to be feared. It means living our sexuality the way God, who invented the whole system, planned it.

Sounds like marriage to me.

Chastity Is Real Love

"Why is chastity so important?"

"What does chastity have to do with finding love?"

Chastity is important for a lot of reasons. It is important because it protects our relationships—with God and with each other. It is important because it helps us to find and to live real love. I honestly believe that chastity is the only way to find love in this love-starved world of ours.

Sexual attraction, at its most basic level, is a human drive, much like hunger or anger. Human drives, by themselves, don't know real love. Drives only know "want what I want when I want it". When you are very hungry and you see a pizza, your drive wants to reach out, grab that pizza and eat it.[2] It is your brain that says, "We are in a restaurant, and that pizza is on someone else's table. Also, the particular slice you are ogling happens to belong to a small child. Don't take it."

Taking the pizza would not be a loving thing, but your drive alone doesn't know that. Your brain has to be the one to break the news. Your brain cannot be very effective, however, if the drive doesn't listen. Your brain and your willpower must be stronger than your drives.

This applies in many different situations. If you are angry, your anger drive may cause you to want to hit someone. It is your brain that says, "Not loving". And when your sex drive says, "Gee, sex would sure be fun right now", it is your brain that has to say "no". It is our brains and our wills that choose to love, not our drives.

Chastity is about developing self-control. It means putting our drives under the control of our brains. Chastity means being able to say "no" when our drives are screaming "Yes!!!".

Chastity helps us to find love in another way. It keeps our brains clear so that we can recognize the right person and get rid of the wrong people.

"Dating chaste" means spending your time doing positive, nonsexual things with this person. It means getting to know this person, spending your time together talking and having fun. It means seeing how this person reacts in different situations and how compatible the two of you are. Chastity means not allowing the emotional bond that sex brings. It means allowing yourself to think clearly. Chastity

---

[2] This is "pizza love" in its purest form.

doesn't mean that you are not sexually attracted to this person. It just means that you are controlling that attraction and not acting on it.

If you date chaste, one of two things will happen. One is that you will be able to look at this person with a clear mind and say, "You get on my nerves. Good-bye."

The other is that, if the relationship is right, something very subtle will begin to develop. There will be a feeling, a realization that may be almost imperceptible at first, but it will grow steadily until you can look at this person and say, "I love you, and I know it is you. There is not a sexual bond here distorting my emotions. I am thinking clearly, and I know that I love you." Believe me, when that happens, it is better than sex. And it will make sex better when the time is right.

Walter Trobisch once pointed out that when an orchestra tunes up, it doesn't start with the drums and the trumpets. It starts with the flutes and the violins, because otherwise the loud trumpets and drums would drown out the quieter instruments.[3] The same applies to sex and love. Love is very delicate and develops very slowly, but premature sex will drown that love in the intensity of sexual passion.

It is easy to want to give in to sexual feelings. They are often at their strongest when we are with someone we care about. But the old saying is true: "Love takes time." Letting our sexual feelings get the best of us can only hurt love. It pays to wait.

---

[3] Walter Trobisch, *I Loved a Girl* (San Francisco: HarperCollins, 1989), p. 8.

Living Together

"What's the matter with my boyfriend and me living together?"

By "living together", I assume you mean "living together and sleeping together". This is a bad idea for several reasons.

First and most obvious—you are not married. You have not made a final, public commitment to each other. God has not joined you together in a sacramental bond. Sex is a renewal of the sacrament, and you have no sacrament to renew. Sex speaks the language of "I have given myself to you forever", not "We'll see how this works out." If you are not married, you are speaking the language of the body in a lie.

Second, and probably because of this, living together before marriage is not good for relationships. Studies consistently show a much higher divorce rate for couples who live together before marriage.

There is a reason for this higher divorce rate. In your sexual activity, you are speaking the language of forever. In this situation, to complicate matters further, you are *acting* married. You share an address and a phone number. You have mingled your possessions. You eat together, clean together and entertain together. You are functioning on all personal and social levels as a married couple.

But you are not married. There is no long-term commitment. The "back door" is always open, because you have deliberately left it open. Either one of you is free to leave at any time. And both of you, somewhere in the back of your minds, know that. This situation causes trouble, for several reasons.

First of all, the lack of permanence keeps everyone on his "best behavior". It is much more difficult to speak up when you know that if things get too rough, the other person may disappear. It becomes much easier to be quiet and to avoid "rocking the boat". In this situation, problems are often repressed instead of expressed, and pressure grows.

Psychologist Laura Schlessinger, in her best-selling book *Ten Stupid Things Women Do to Mess up Their Lives*, says that men and women often have very different reasons for wanting to live together. For women, living together is often about "auditioning" for the role of wife. They see it as a first step—a way to convince their boyfriends that they should get married. But this is bad strategy. She says that moving in with a man without a commitment tells him that he doesn't have to do much to get you. If you are dating a "commitment-phobe", someone who is afraid to make a permanent commitment to marriage, moving in with him will make him *less* motivated to commit. Now he doesn't *have* to get married. He already has all of the benefits without having to make the commitment. [4]

Women often move in with men in order to be protected and nurtured. Without a commitment, however, that security isn't real. It is an illusion. The man and the "security"

[4] Laura Schlessinger, *Ten Stupid Things Women Do to Mess up Their Lives* (New York: Harper Perennial, 1995), p. 99.

can vanish at any time. That uncertainty creates vulnerability and tension.

Many couples live together as a sort of "trial marriage" to decide if they are compatible enough to spend the rest of their lives together. This, however, is a very bad way to make a marriage decision. To make a decision this important you need to be objective, and objectivity is the last thing you have when you cohabitate. You have a vested interest in staying together. You are speaking the language of forever with your bodies and blurring your ability to make a good decision. To make matters worse, you have already made your home with him. Whatever short-term desires you may have had for nurturing or security are now being met right here at home, from a person to whom you have given yourself. In this situation, leaving becomes much more difficult.

When so much of your security is tied up in "making it work" with this person, it becomes easy to lose perspective. You worry so much about "how can I make him stay?" that you forget to ask the question you are supposed to be asking: "Is this the person I want to stay with for the rest of my life?"

People who live together often tend, on the whole, to be less mature than those who wait until they are married to cohabitate. They tend to be more interested in gratifying their short-term desires for sex or security than they are in going carefully through the steps necessary to build a committed, permanent relationship.

When you are ready to make a commitment to building a home and a life together, make that commitment. But don't try to do it halfway. It doesn't work.

Sexual Compatibility

"Do you think it is okay to have a strong sexual relationship before you get married and live together? So you can find out if you are right for each other before getting married."

I love this question.

I suppose it makes sense to ask a question like this if you believe what society tells you about sex. If sex is the greatest thing that will ever happen to you, and if some people are "better" at sex than others, then wouldn't it be fair to find out if this person is "good" at sex before signing on the dotted line, especially if this is the only person you'll ever have sex with?

But look at it from the other side. How would you like it if someone said, "I love you. You are my best friend, my partner, my soul mate. I want to spend the rest of my life with you. I want to share children with you. I want to grow old with you. But first, we are going to have a little sex test. And if you don't score[5] at least a B+ or A−, the wedding is off." How would that make you feel?

It is a mistake to believe that "good sex" is about technique. Good sex is about good relationships. If a husband and wife have a good marriage, if they get along well and have real emotional intimacy, if they trust each other and look out for each other, their sex life will reflect that. If they are fighting, if they are inconsiderate, if there is no trust or intimacy, or if one of them is cheating, their mari-

---

[5] Pardon the pun.

103

tal sex will suffer. The "quality" of their sex life is a direct reflection of the quality of their intimacy and the quality of their marriage.

The beauty of marital sex is that you don't have to "get it right" the first time. You have a lifetime to practice, to learn together, and to give yourselves to each other. What a great learning environment—being with one sexual partner you trust—someone who is not ever going to leave you. As long as your relationship and your emotional intimacy grow, sex will get better, not worse, as the years go by.

Two friends of mine married each other a few years ago. When they were engaged, her friends at work were telling her about all the tests they should have to make sure neither of them had a sexually transmitted disease. "We don't need them", she said. "We're both virgins."

After her coworkers recovered from their shock, one of them said, "You mean you can't compare each other to anyone else? Your sex life is gonna be *great!*"

Engagement

"Why is it damaging to have sex with someone you're engaged to?"

"Okay", you say. "We did it your way. We dated chaste, we allowed that feeling to develop all on its own. Now we *know* we're in love. Can we do it now? What difference does a piece of paper make when we know we are committed to each other for life?"

The answer is no—the Church says that couples must wait until they are *married*, not just engaged. Why? Isn't the Church being a little too nitpicky on this point?

Believe it or not, there are very good reasons for this requirement. First of all, engagement is still a time of trial. You are still learning about this person. You are not fully committed. Half of all engagements break off. But it is much more difficult to break off an engagement if there is a bond or a pregnancy.

The other reason goes a little deeper. Sex during engagement might make more sense if God weren't involved. Then we could just decide for ourselves what constitutes a permanent commitment. (Signing a mortgage? Merging checking accounts?) But God *is* involved, especially in marriage. Sex isn't designed to be *just* an expression of love. Remember how we talked about the fact that sex is how God brings new life into the world, and He is actually, tangibly present when a husband and wife come together that way? Sex is God's in a very unique way.

God designed sex to be a renewal of the marriage covenant—a renewal of the sacrament. Sacraments, you may remember from your catechism class, give us grace—strength and help from God. That sacrament is renewed, and the grace of the sacrament of marriage is poured out, each time a husband and wife come together in marital sexual intercourse.

But what if you are not married yet? How can you renew a sacrament you haven't received? The sacrament of marriage is similar to ordination for a priest. In the sacrament of holy orders, a priest receives the power to consecrate the host. But can a priest consecrate the host a week before his ordination? A day before? Is there such thing as "preordination consecration"? No. And, in the same way, there should be no such thing, spiritually, as "premarital sex". The power flows from the sacrament.

Believe it or not, there are practical benefits to abstaining when you are engaged. For one thing, you find out how strong your fiancé's self-control is. If this person can control his sexual desire around you when you are both madly in love and wanting to spend the rest of your lives together, you learn a few things. You learn that this person can delay immediate gratification for the sake of someone else. You learn that he takes God and His commands seriously. And you learn that this person will have self-control around *other* people after you are married.

Sometimes God's rules seem arbitrary, and none seems more so than the "no sex during engagement" rule. But isn't it amazing how beautiful His rules turn out to be when we finally understand them? I've learned that it pays to trust Him.

"Are you still sinning if you have only been with one partner and marry him?"

This is closely related to the "If we make a mistake and do it, should we get married?" question we discussed earlier.

At the time you had sex with this person, you were not married. You had no way of knowing with absolute certainty that this would be the person you would marry. You had no way of knowing for certain that this would be the only person you would give yourself to. Sex doesn't speak the language of "maybe we'll get married later", or even "we'll probably get married later." It says, "We *are* married." So doing it outside of marriage is speaking the language in a lie. That is a sin, regardless of what happens afterward. Sin cannot be retroactive. The sin is in what you did at the time, not about what you do or do not do afterward.

Is Sex Bad or Great?

"Why is sex considered to be something bad when it is known to be one of the greatest experiences in our lives?"

There are a lot of great experiences in life. Accomplishing a goal, experiencing real love, making a difference in someone's life, encountering God, giving birth—these are all great experiences.

Sex, in and of itself, is not going to be the greatest experience in your life, I assure you. Sex is great—really and truly great in every sense of the word—only when it is honestly expressing what it means. Sex is great when your mind and heart and relationship and life all say the same thing: "I love you; I am sacramentally united to you; I give myself to you forever; I want to share children with you."

That is great.

"Choice"

"Why are women who have sex criticized by the Catholic Church? Isn't it their choice whether or not they want to or are ready?"

I have never heard the Catholic Church "criticize" women, or anyone else, for having sex. What the Church says, in a nutshell, is this: "God created sex to be expressed in a certain context, and if you take it out of that context, you could be hurt very badly. We love you and don't want you to have to experience that pain."

The Church's message is a message of love and concern, not of criticism or condemnation.

One-Night Stands

"What is wrong with a one-night stand?"

Everything. A one-night stand is speaking to someone you barely know in the language of forever, self-giving love. It makes a mockery of the language of sex. It is a lie of the highest order. It is putting yourself and another person at extremely high risk of pregnancy and sexually transmitted diseases. It is destroying your ability to bond with your spouse later in life. It is committing a sin and participating in someone else's sin.

All that for a few minutes of pleasure? Don't bother—a one-night stand is definitely not worth it.

Marriage—Just for Sex?

"Is it okay to get married just to have sex?"

Not a good idea. Sex is an expression of married *love*, not just "marriage". The thrill of sex without love wears off very quickly, and you are left spending the rest of your life with someone you are probably not particularly thrilled about.

Remarriage

"If your husband dies and if you get remarried, is it a sin to have sex?"

No. Marriage means giving yourself to someone "til death do us part". If your spouse dies, you have been parted. You are free to remarry and to "give yourself" to that person.

Single Adults

"If you are an adult (about thirty-two) and are in a relationship, would it be that bad to have sex?"

I am an adult. I am single. I doubt the questioner realized it, but I am a living expert on this particular question.

I am not asking you to do anything I don't do myself. The rules are the same regardless of age. Chastity is not about how old you are or how mature you are. It is about your state in life. Sex outside marriage has certain consequences, and those consequences are the same whether you are fifteen, thirty-five or fifty-five.[6] Sex outside of marriage puts yourself and another person at risk. It is using, and there is no "magical" age when you suddenly have a license to use another person.

Never Married—No Sex?

"What if you don't want ever to get married? Can you never have sex?"

Sex speaks the language of marriage. It says, "I give myself to you totally and completely, forever." The heart hears that language, no matter what. To speak it outside the context of a permanent relationship is to tell a lie with your body and to use the other person. Sex outside marriage is "pizza love".

When does it suddenly become okay to speak that language when you don't mean it—to use another person— just because you have decided not to marry and you want to know what sex is like? Never.

If you don't want to give your life to someone, you could never fully experience sex anyway. What makes sex

---

[6] I know, a fifty-five-year-old can't get pregnant. But she can get an STD, she can bond, and she can turn away from God.

truly great is speaking the language honestly, not just going through the motions with someone because it feels good for you or because you want to see what it is like.

Contrary to popular belief, sex is not a need. Millions of unmarried people live extremely happy lives without it, and when they die, it isn't celibacy that kills them.

Marital Chastity

"Do married people have to live chastity?"

The beauty of chastity is that it is not a "do as I say, not as I do" kind of virtue. Chastity is for everyone—married people, single people—even priests and nuns.

Chastity does not mean "don't have sex". Chastity means understanding that sex speaks a language—the language of permanent, forever, "I give myself to you" self-donating love and of living that way.

For single people, obviously, chastity means abstaining from sex. But what does chastity mean for married people?

Getting married does not just mean that you can suddenly do anything you want to your husband or wife. Marital sex is "making love" in the most real sense. It says, "I give myself to you, and to what is best for you, forever." Chastity for married people means respecting that language. It means speaking it honestly at all times. Chastity means making sure that, in your marital sexual language, you are looking out for what is best for your spouse. Saying, "I want sex, I want it now, and I don't care what you want" is not a loving thing to do. It is not chastity.

John Paul II made a statement a few years back that caused a big stir. He said that there should not be "lust" in the relationship between husband and wife. The U.S. press used the quote to try to make him a laughingstock. They said that the Pope believed that there should not be sexual attraction between a husband and a wife and that spouses should not enjoy sex.

If the press had listened to everything else he said, they would have realized how wrong they were. "Lust" doesn't mean sexual attraction. Attraction, especially between a husband and a wife, is a good thing. John Paul II has said that himself many times. Lust, on the other hand, means reducing the whole person to sex *alone*. Lust is the will to *use* another person—to see that person as merely an object of personal, sexual satisfaction. And there is no place for that, even in marriage.

Husbands and wives should love each other. They should cherish each other. They should care for each other. They should have a healthy, active, enjoyable sexual relationship. But they should never, ever use each other. Using is not a chaste thing to do.

The Church and Contraception

"Why does the Church not condone contraceptives for people who don't want many children?"

This is the second part of chastity for married people—a part that, unfortunately, very few Catholics understand.

The Catholic Church teaches that it is wrong to use *artificial* birth control. Most people think that this is because the Church wants everyone to have fourteen children so that they can grow up and get rich and put money in the collection and the Church can get rich and take over the world.

This is not the case.

Sex is the act that God uses to perform his favorite act— bringing new life into the world, new human beings who are created in His image and likeness, destined to live forever. That fact alone gives sex an incredible dignity. This also makes sex "God's" in a very specific and unique way. When a man and a woman come together in sex, God is *there*, prepared to perform His most creative act.

But in all forms of artificial birth control, we change sex somehow. We reroute it. In doing that, we "block God out". We change His act, and, in doing that, we tell Him we don't want Him around this time.

Sex is an amazing language of self-gift, a way for spouses to say to each other with their bodies, "I give myself completely to you, and I accept you completely as you are." But artificial contraception changes that language. It says, "I accept *most* of you, but I am sorry—your fertility is not on the acceptable list. It will have to go before I take you." In artificial contraception, we don't give ourselves totally or accept each other totally.

My friend Janet Smith demonstrates the difference this way. She says that if you made a list of each member of the opposite sex with whom you wouldn't mind spending an exciting weekend in the Bahamas, you would probably have a fairly long list. But if you made a list of people you would want to join with in having and raising a child, that list would be considerably shorter.

In contraceptive sex, you are saying, "I want to have fun with you, but I don't necessarily want any consequences." Noncontraceptive sex, on the other hand, says "I give myself to you, and if a child results from our union, that would be great, because I will be here with you to love and to raise that child."

Most married people who use contraception, to be sure, do not intend to speak this kind of language. They love each other, and they are doing what they believe to be best for themselves and their families. They are, however, speaking the language of sexuality in a lie, even if they don't realize it. Many couples who switch from artificial to natural methods of birth control report that when they were using artificial contraceptives, they could sense that something wasn't right, even if they couldn't identify exactly what it was. It was only after they switched to the natural methods that they could identify the problem. The language is the language, even if we only hear it subconsciously.

Interestingly enough, some women understand this difference in language, even if they don't acknowledge that they do. A study of women who have abortions found that many were aware of their contraceptive options but freely chose not to use them. Many of the reasons they gave revolved around issues like "forcing a definition of the relationship".[7] Janet Smith concludes that, "Their careless

---

[7] Kristen Luker, *Taking Chances: Abortion and the Decision Not to Contracept* (Berkeley, 1975), p. 70.

114

use of contraceptives is precisely their desire to engage in meaningful sexual activity rather than meaningless sexual activity."[8] This conclusion is borne out among the young teenagers I speak to who tell me that they have sex with their boyfriends without using contraceptives, but they believe it is okay because "we love each other."

The Church isn't saying that married couples must have as many children as is biologically possible. She is just saying that there is a right way and a wrong way to go about spacing children, and changing the act of sex to suit our purposes is the wrong way.

"If Catholics don't encourage birth control, what else can people do?"

When God created sex, He knew what He was doing. He knew that it would bring new life into the world, and He knew that raising that life would be a tremendous responsibility. He knew that different couples would have different capacities to raise children and that some could handle more children than others.

He made women's bodies, therefore, in such a way that they could get pregnant only a few days a month. This way, women can make love to their husbands without getting pregnant every single time. God also created women's bodies so that they would give very clear signs when conception could occur. He also gave us the brains to figure out what those signs are.

---

[8] Janet Smith, "The Connection between Contraception and Abortion", *Homiletic and Pastoral Review*, April 1993, p. 14.

In previous generations, Catholic couples used a method known as "rhythm", where they would chart the woman's menstrual cycles on a calendar and use that information to guess when she would be fertile in the future. That system worked fairly well, about as well as the artificial methods like the condom that were available at that time.

Now, scientists have discovered far more reliable methods of determining fertility. These methods are called Natural Family Planning, or NFP. A woman's body gives very clear signs when she is fertile—her body temperature rises, and the quality and quantity of her cervical mucus changes. In modern methods of NFP, a woman looks for and charts these signs. By abstaining on the days she is fertile, a couple can avoid pregnancy during times when they are unprepared for another baby—because money is tight, or one of them is ill or exhausted, or because for whatever reason they don't feel they are prepared to take on responsibility for another life.

NFP is great because it completely respects each partner. It says, "I love you and accept you totally as you are. If you are fertile and a pregnancy would not be good for you right now, I will find another way to show my love for you." That is an act of amazing love.

Artificial Insemination

"What do you think about artificial insemination?"

I think, and the Catholic Church teaches, that artificial insemination is wrong, for several reasons.

We have talked a lot in this book about God's plan that new life come into the world through the committed love of a father and a mother. The sexual act, their act of unity and self-gift, is the act that brings that new life into the world.

Artificial insemination turns that all upside down. Children don't result from love but from a laboratory experiment. Either sperm or an egg is often taken from a "donor", depriving those donors of children who are theirs and creating legal nightmares in which the children become pawns. In some cases, eggs are fertilized, creating new human beings with souls, and then those tiny new human beings are left in "cold storage" for years or even indefinitely. This is not leading to respect for life. This is turning the creation of life into a big, dangerous game.

There is another reason to oppose artificial insemination. When insemination is attempted, several eggs are "harvested" at once. The technicians attempt to fertilize all of them. Then, when more than one egg is fertilized, one is chosen to be implanted, and the rest are "destroyed". Remember, when a human egg is fertilized, a new human being has come into existence. These new human beings are being destroyed by the thousands in insemination laboratories.

For us to be randomly creating and destroying people is tantamount to playing God. We have no right.

Divorce and Annulment

"Why doesn't the Catholic Church allow divorce?"

It is true, the Catholic Church doesn't recognize divorce, because she says marriage is permanent. But that statement is not a "rule"—it is just a description.

Christ said, "What God has joined together, let no man put asunder" (Mk 10:9). What He is saying here is that, in marriage, God joins people together for life. He actually makes the two into one. He binds their souls together. And no one, not even the Catholic Church, is powerful enough to break that bond. It can't be done.

The Church doesn't make up power. She only has the power that God gives to her. So the Church isn't saying "We won't give divorces." She is saying, "We *can't*. God didn't give us the power to take apart what He puts together." He didn't give that kind of power to *anyone*, not even His Church.

None of this means that a Catholic can't stop living with a spouse if the situation calls for that. If the spouse is abusive, addicted to drugs or alcohol, bad for the children or in some other way dangerous to live with, moving out is the best solution. Likewise, there is nothing technically immoral about a Catholic obtaining a legal divorce. All the Church is saying is that even though the couple has been legally divorced, the spiritual bond is still there, so neither can marry again unless the first spouse dies or they obtain an annulment.

"If the Church doesn't allow divorce, why do people get annulments? Isn't that just a Catholic divorce?"

An annulment doesn't say that two people were married and now they are not married. An annulment says that, for some reason, a marriage never took place to begin with.

In marriage, a man and a woman are agreeing to something very specific. They are agreeing to remain married forever. They are agreeing to be completely faithful to each other. And they are agreeing to be open to having children. If someone is standing on the altar thinking, "If this doesn't work out, I'll leave and marry someone else", or "I can still keep my other boyfriend", or "There is no way I ever want children", that person is not agreeing to marriage, and no marriage is taking place. God is not uniting the couple sacramentally. He is not binding their souls together.

When a couple applies for an annulment, they go to a marriage tribunal. That tribunal looks back at what was going on at the time of the couple's wedding to see if an actual marriage took place. They interview each partner, and other people who knew them then, to find out what their attitudes were toward the marriage. If either was not committing to a real marriage, or was for some reason not *able* freely to make a commitment (severe immaturity, emotional or mental illness, coercion, and so on), the tribunal declares that no marriage existed, and the people are free to marry others. Their marriage hasn't been dissolved. On the spiritual level, it never existed in the first place.

"My parents got an annulment. If they were never married, does that make me illegitimate?"

No, no, no. Illegitimacy is strictly a *legal* term. It refers to a child who was born when its parents were not legally married. Legitimacy is important only in determining inheritance and in helping royal families decide who gets to be called a "prince" and who doesn't.

Annulment, on the other hand, is a moral term. It does not say that a *legal* marriage did not take place in the eyes of the state. As far as the law is concerned, the two people were married. Annulment just says that, in God's eyes, the couple was never sacramentally joined together.

Even in the eyes of the Church, a marriage is presumed to be valid until a tribunal definitely determines that it is not. This means that you were born into a legal marriage that was presumed spiritually valid at the time of your birth.

I think the whole concept of "legitimacy", even from a legal standpoint, is too easily misunderstood. It gives people value based, not on who they are, but on the circumstances of their birth. And that is wrong.

In God's eyes, there is no such thing as an "illegitimate" person. We are all "legitimate" because we were created in His image and likeness, and He is madly in love with each and every one of us.

Don't worry. Both legally and spiritually, you are as "legitimate" as anyone else in this world.

Homosexuality

"What causes homosexuality?"

Nobody knows for sure why some people are sexually attracted to people of the same sex. Some people think it is caused by genetics or prenatal hormones or some other cause that existed at birth. Other people believe that the cause of homosexuality is developmental or environmental —that the homosexual orientation happens as a result of factors that existed in the person's early life.

There has been a lot of attention lately on studies that suggest a gene might possibly cause homosexuality—the so-called "gay gene". The media has often given the impression that this theory has been proven and that homosexuality is definitely caused by genetics. But the experts I've spoken with tell me this is by no means the case. They say theories that the homosexual orientation exists from birth have very little scientific foundation.[9]

John Harvey, O.S.F.S., noted theologian and expert on homosexuality, sums it up best. He says that "Some theories say there are biological or genetic causes, or even hormones in the preborn child, but these theories have little scientific foundation. They fail to consider the environmental factors of very early life. Other theories hold that the

---

[9] Shortly after the release of the last major study on genetics and homosexuality, I had the privilege of speaking with the great geneticist Jérôme Lejeune, who is famous for having discovered the genetic cause of Down's Syndrome. I asked him about the possibility of a gene responsible for homosexuality. He said that it had not been proven, and furthermore he didn't believe it ever would be. He didn't believe that homosexuality was a genetic trait.

psychological factors of early life are far more important than any—still unknown—homosexual gene."[10]

"I have heard that the Church is against homosexuality. If so, why are some homosexuals still Catholic?"

Okay—this is a very important distinction. There is a difference between having a homosexual orientation and engaging in homosexual activity. Having a homosexual orientation just means that a person is sexually attracted primarily to people of his own sex. It is not something he chooses but rather something that has happened to him. Homosexual activity, on the other hand, means actually doing sexual things with someone of the same sex.

The Church is not, repeat, *not* against *people* who have this orientation or any other people. Remember that *everyone* is created in the image and likeness of God and that He is madly in love with every single person He created. That includes *all* people who have a homosexual orientation. The Church is Christ's presence on earth. Our job, then, is the same; to love *each and every person* with the love of Christ.

As we discussed in the last question, no one really knows exactly why some people develop a sexual attraction to people of the same sex. Some theories say that there are biological or genetic causes, other say a homosexual orientation is developmental, happening as a result of circumstances in a person's early life.

---

[10] John Harvey, O.S.F.S., personal correspondence, 1996.

Either way, it is not a sin to be attracted to someone of the same sex. It can't be a sin, because it isn't freely chosen. A sin is something a person decides to do. An attraction, whether to the same sex or to the opposite sex, is something that happens involuntarily, not something chosen.

The Church is, however, opposed to homosexual *activity* —doing sexual things with someone of the same sex. This opposition comes, not out of condemnation, but out of love and concern for the persons involved. Homosexual activity is dangerous to those who practice it, on several levels. It is obviously dangerous physically. AIDS has killed hundreds of thousands of homosexual men in the past fifteen years. The condom is even less effective in homosexual activity than it is in heterosexual activity. Homosexual activity can also lead to other diseases.

Homosexual activity is also dangerous spiritually. God designed sex to be used in the context of marriage, for a man and a woman to give themselves to each other and bring a family into the world. To use the sexual function any other way is a sin. All sin, including homosexual activity, cuts a person off from God. It is choosing our own way over His way. Morality is God's instruction manual, and going against it hurts us and hurts our relationship with Him.

People who have a homosexual orientation are, in one way, no different from the rest of us. Because of original sin, we are all inclined, in one way or another, to be attracted to activities that are sinful. For some people, that attraction may be to abusing substances like drugs or alcohol. For others, it may be to heterosexual abuses of the gift of sexuality. The person with a homosexual orientation has to fight temptation in the same way we all do.

People with a homosexual orientation are called to live chastity just like the rest of us. There are thousands upon thousands of men and women in the Church who are striving to do just that, despite a homosexual orientation. There is even an organization called Courage that is dedicated to supporting these men and women and to helping them grow in chastity and holiness. For more information on Courage, see the resource list in Appendix 2 at the end of this book.

There are others in the Church who want to live unchaste lives unapologetically and still be full, active members of the Church. They are trying to have it both ways. Christ said, "If you love me, keep my commandments." The Church teaches very clearly that homosexual activity is a serious sin. Again, the Church doesn't make these teachings up. She teaches with the authority of Christ. Those teachings will not change.

"How do you feel about gay people?"

There are two answers to that question. The first is the fact that *all* people are created in the image and likeness of God and are loved by God, and that includes people who, for whatever reason, have a homosexual orientation. He doesn't love them less when they are sinning and more when they are not. He loves them madly, all the time, and, *because* He loves them He wants them to stop sinning. I recognize that these people are God's creation, created in

His image and likeness. They are human persons, creatures of God. I love them, and I want what is best for them.

There are also people I know *personally*, people I consider my friends, people who are extremely important in my life, who for whatever reason have a homosexual orientation. I love them as children of God, but I also love them personally, as *friends*. It is out of genuine love and personal affection that I care very deeply about these people, and I worry *very much* about their physical, emotional and spiritual well-being. I don't want anything bad to happen to any of them. I want them to live long, healthy, fulfilling lives and to spend eternity with their Creator. I would be absolutely devastated to lose any of them.

"If the Church really loves gay people, why don't we want them to find love and to be happy?"

Good question. Of course we want them to be happy. But is that *all* that love means—wanting someone to be "happy" right now? Of course not. Heterosexual sex outside of marriage might make a couple "happy" for a while, but it will make their lives much more difficult in the long run. Eating a lot makes me happy for a while, but I generally regret it in a few hours. There are a lot of things that make us *happy* in the short run but aren't best for us in the long run.

We have been talking throughout this book about how real love means wanting what is *best* for someone, in every way. We have also been talking about sexual activity and how, outside the context of marriage, it can be extremely damaging and *definitely* not in a person's best interest.

The same is true for persons with a homosexual orientation. The homosexual lifestyle may make them "happy" for a while, but that happiness comes at a price. They face serious physical, emotional and spiritual consequences. Their short-term "happiness" isn't worth the long-term risks.

"Why can't gay people get married if they love each other?"

To understand this question, we need to understand what marriage is. Remember, we didn't invent sex and marriage —God did. He created them together, right back there at the beginning of time. He did that because sex and marriage go together—for a reason. Sex is not an expression of just any kind of love—it is an expression of permanent, exclusive, self-giving love between a man and a woman. Married sexual love is the kind of love that is the foundation of a family.

Sexual intercourse is, by definition, an act that occurs between a man and a woman. If you know anything about biology, you know that the parts are designed to work together. In sexual arousal, the male and female sexual organs "prepare" for each other, to put it delicately. In joining together, they complete each other. They become one. The man gives, the woman receives. His body is designed to manufacture sperm. Her body is designed to receive it and possibly to lead it to a waiting egg. A doctor once told me that female sexual satisfaction is in part tied to her body receiving and absorbing semen and that her body is even designed to come to recognize and accept one man's sperm and to tend to reject other sperm.

None of this happens in homosexual activity. It may be "sexual" in the sense of using the sexual organs, but it is not sexual in the true sense of the word—in this complementary act of total sexual completion, according to the complementary design of our bodies.

Marriage is the context for which God designed sexual intercourse. He created sex in marriage to be a complete joining of male and female—physically, emotionally and spiritually. This joining of male and female would be the foundation for a family—the arena through which He would bring new life into the world. The sexual act would be not only a sign of their love but a sign of the life-giving and constantly fruitful love of God. It would be their participation in His love. Sexual intercourse is, by definition, an act between a man and a woman, expressing this fruitful, life-giving love of God.

Marriage is then also, by definition, the union of a man and a woman. That's what it is. That's the way God designed it.

People with a homosexual orientation are, technically, free to get married. But marriage is, by definition, to a member of the opposite sex, which is not what they want. It is also, of course, a very bad idea for someone with a homosexual orientation to marry. It isn't fair to the opposite-sex spouse.

But the solution is not to attempt "same-sex marriages". We could pretend they are married. The state could pretend they are married. But we didn't invent marriage, and the state didn't invent marriage. God did. He decides who is married and who isn't. And He created marriage, just as He created sex, to be between a male and a female.

Same-sex "marriage", then, wouldn't be marriage at all. It would just be a license to misuse the gift of sexuality.

"How come some people are so sensitive about 'gay jokes'? What's the big deal?"

The "deal" is very, very big. Imagine being someone with a homosexual orientation. You didn't ask for this to happen to you, you probably didn't want it to happen to you. Now you are trying to figure out what to do about it. Like everyone else, you have a need to give and to receive real love. But where? Do you stay in the Church? Is there a place for you there? Does anyone love you? Who really cares about you?

Then you are with a group of "Christians" or "Catholics" who don't know about your struggle, and you hear them saying things like, "I hate fags" or "I wish they all would die", or telling cruel, mean-spirited jokes. What are you going to think? You will think, "Well, obviously these people don't love me. I'll look for love somewhere else." That is how many people end up in radical "gay rights" groups. They are looking for acceptance.

You, as a Christian, have a big responsibility. You represent the Church. What you do reflects on the Church. The way people see you is the way they see the Church. If you are cruel or insensitive, you will drive people away, not only from you, but from the Church as well. You are responsible for that. If you have knowingly or unknowingly driven someone away from Christ's Church, you will have to answer for it on Judgment Day.

Don't take this lightly. Your obligation to love is serious, and it applies to everyone you meet.

"What if I'm gay?"

First of all, if you are a teenager, it is not unusual to ask this question. Nearly every teenager on the face of the earth at some point fears having a homosexual orientation. This kind of fear in adolescence is perfectly normal. Adolescence is a time of tremendous upheaval. You are moving from the "homoerotic stage" (it isn't dirty—it just means that same-sex friendships are the most important relationships in your life) to the "heteroerotic stage" (where opposite-sex relationships become more important). In the meantime, you are going through rapid sexual development. You still have important same-sex role models, but sometimes that admiration or attraction can become sexualized in some way. In other words, it is very easy to get your wires crossed for a while. Your sexual attractions will be very erratic. "Crushes" or infatuation with someone of the same sex are normal at this stage. This kind of crush— or even an experience with homosexual activity—does not prove that someone has a homosexual orientation. Only an extremely small percentage of people actually become adults with such an exclusively homosexual orientation.

Relax. It will all sort itself out over time. Many experts say that, with all of the upheaval of adolescence, no one below the age of twenty-five or so can be absolutely certain of a homosexual orientation.[11] The best thing you can do

---

[11] John Harvey, O.S.F.S., *The Homosexual Person* (San Francisco: Ignatius Press, 1988), p. 189.

is to concentrate on yourself, build healthy relationships with God and with people of both sexes, and become the best person you possibly can. If you don't feel like dating, don't date. A lot of people don't. If confusion about your sexual attractions is really bothering you, make an appointment to talk about it with a good Christian counselor or therapist.[12]

Most importantly, whatever your sexual attractions or inclinations, don't act on them. Understand them as a part of the confusion of a developing sexual identity, and then go play basketball or something.

If, however, you are no longer a teenager, and you are one of the small percentage of people who, by your mid-twenties, still experience sexual attraction primarily to people of your own sex, you should take this seriously. You need to talk to someone. Please call one of the numbers listed in the back of this book.

If you are a person with a homosexual orientation, please know this: This is not the end of the world. You are a person created in the image and likeness of God. He loves you. Anyone who truly follows Him loves you too. Please don't leave His Church or go into the "gay lifestyle" thinking it will fulfill you. I don't believe that it will. There is no real fulfillment apart from God. There is a spiritual "God-shaped hole" inside each of us, and that void at the center of our lives can be filled only by Him. Let Him fill it for you.

---

[12] Note: Whenever seeing any therapist, counselor or psychologist, make sure that this person understands and accepts the Church's teachings—especially on sexuality.

6

Finding Real Love

Not Worthy of Real Love?

"So many of us are conditioned by our experiences in society to believe that we aren't worthy of the 'real' love you describe that turning to sex to fill that emptiness seems like all we have. My first thought on hearing you was that no one will ever love me that much."

Many people think there is more extramarital sexual activity today because people have less self-control, or because they are curious or bored.

I disagree. There may be some people who fall into that category, but I believe that, for most people, the real reasons go far deeper—back to the reasons described above.

Single people of all ages are engaging in sex because they are looking for love. After all, the world as it is today offers most of us very little real, honest love. Love, however, is a real need. We were created to give it and to receive it. That needs runs very, very deep. For those who find no love in their lives, there is a powerful temptation to turn to sex to try to fill the void. Society tells us that we will find love in sex. Why else would songs use the terms "love", "in love", "make love" and "sex" almost interchangeably? Why would people on TV or in a movie instantly fall into bed with anyone they find remotely attractive? Sex must be the place to find love, right?

It doesn't work that way. Sex doesn't "make" love, it doesn't "cause" love, and it doesn't "lead to" love. Sex is sex, and if there was no love before the sex, there probably won't be any afterward. In fact, as we have already discussed, sex in an uncommitted relationship can cause pressure and actually damage love.

Many couples who get involved sexually really do love each other. I am not questioning that. They may not *mean* to be using each other. But they are clearly not thinking about what they are doing. They are putting each other at risk, and they are putting their relationship at risk. That is not loving.

Real love comes from a much deeper place. It comes from understanding our own dignity as created in the image and likeness of God, and that means holding out for someone else who will understand and respect that dignity, too.

Many people feel that "no one will ever love me like that"—that they are somehow unworthy of real love. The solution for someone like that is not to settle for counterfeit love but to strive to understand how all of us, as human beings, hold the incredible dignity of being created in the image and likeness of God. Only then can we understand *why* we are worthy of real love, and why we should not allow ourselves to be used. Once we see that dignity, we realize that we should not settle for "pizza love". We need to hold out for the real thing.

Finding Mr. or Ms. Right

"How do you know you've met the love of your life?"

"How do you know when you are in love?"

In the movies, people know exactly when they are in love. They look into each others' eyes, and time stands still. The music begins to play, and *boom*, they are in love. As soon as they hear that music, they know it must be time to fall in love.

Unfortunately, real life doesn't work that way. Our lives don't have soundtracks, and it takes a lot more than a couple of verses of a song for real love to develop.

Being "in love" does not mean "I get a warm, wonderful feeling around you", or "I am very sexually attracted to you." It means "I want to share the rest of my life with you. I want to have children with you. I want to grow old with you. I want to marry you." Sexual attraction and wonderful feelings are a part of that, but they are not the whole story.

"In love" is more than just a feeling. It is also a decision. This is important, so I am going to repeat it: *"In love" is not just a feeling—it is a decision.*

The love of your life is, or should be, the person you marry. This is obviously a very important decision, and it should not be based simply on how you "feel". Feelings can come and go for a lot of different reasons, ranging from your emotional state to your choice of breakfast food. Your feelings alone don't know how to make good long-term decisions. They need the help and cooperation of your brain.

I think a lot of people spend a lot of time trying to "define" their feelings—trying to decide if they are "in love" or just "in like" or whatever. Unless you are considering marrying someone, this is a waste of time. "In love" is a decision. It is a part of the marriage decision. Until you are making that kind of decision, don't worry about naming your relationships. Just enjoy them.

"How will I know when I've met the person I should marry?"

The choice of a marriage partner should not be based on "I get a warm, wonderful feeling whenever we're together, and I want to have that warm, wonderful feeling forever, so let's get married." Feelings, as we have discussed, have no logic of their own. They need to be acknowledged, of course, but they need considerable assistance from your brain.

Marriage means choosing the person you will spend the rest of your life with. This, as you may have guessed, is a very long time to spend with one person. This person will live with you, eat meals with you, sleep with you, and go on vacation with you. More important yet, this person will share your children. You need to choose wisely. The decision should not be made based on feelings alone. You need to ask yourself some tough questions. The decision has to be based on solid considerations.

Will this person be a good partner? Is she mature enough to put her own selfish desires aside to look out for what is best for the family? Is he prepared to be a good provider? What is his track record? Is he responsible enough to get a good job and keep it?

Will this person be a good parent? Can you stand the thought of your children turning out *exactly* like this person? They will, you know. Children spend a lot of time with their parents and consequently pick up many or most of their parents' character traits. You had better like your spouse's traits a *lot*, because you will be seeing them again in your children.

If something were to happen to you, would you completely trust this person, *alone*, with the task of raising and forming your children? This is not a pleasant thought, but it is an important consideration. Not everyone dies at a ripe old age with great-grandchildren gathered around the bed. Sometimes a parent dies and leaves young children in the care of the other parent. If you feel that you would need to be around to correct or lessen this person's influence on your children, you are considering the wrong person.

Does this person share your faith in God? God does not give us children so that we can mold them into the coolest, most popular people in school. Our job is to get them to heaven. To do that, we need to raise them believing in God and in His Church. It's tough to do that when only one parent believes. Saying "This is right and this is wrong, and I want you to ignore Mommy until you are thirty-five" does not work. Small children ask about eighty skillion questions in a single day. The answers to those questions go a long way toward forming the kind of adults they will become. Who will be answering those questions for your children?

Does this person you are marrying have sexual self-control? Single people sometimes have this idea that marriage is just some kind of lifelong sex festival and that as long as they have each other, they will never be tempted by other people. Wrong. There are times in every marriage when one partner or the other is sexually unavailable —illness, the last months of pregnancy, travel. There are also times when spouses just get on each others' nerves. At times like this, other people can seem *very* appealing. That can be dangerous, because there are plenty of very attractive people out there who are willing to make themselves available to married men and women. Do you want to marry someone who has never said "no" to sex? If he is not good at saying "no" at eighteen, it won't be any different at forty. Do you want to worry about whether or not your spouse is being faithful? What kind of marriage can you have with someone you couldn't trust on a business trip?

These are very important questions, and if you are not comfortable with all of the answers, you should definitely not marry this person.

None of this is to say that feelings play no role at all in a marriage decision. You don't have to say, "Well, I suppose you would make a good spouse and parent, so even though I don't particularly like you I guess I'll marry you." You need to be happy and excited about the prospect of spending your life with someone. Your brain, however, must also acknowledge this person as a good catch.

Don't listen to your heart alone or your head alone. Wait until your heart and your head agree.

In Love but Miserable?

"My boyfriend and I have been together for a long time. I don't think he'd be the best person for me to marry, but my feelings for him are *so* strong!! Every time I try to break it off, I'm miserable until I go back to him. Am I in love with him? What should I do? *Help!!*"

It is very painful to have strong feelings for someone but to know that this person isn't right for you, or that this person doesn't treat you the way you should be treated, or that the relationship isn't going to work out. It can be difficult to break up—you're miserable in the relationship but even more miserable when you get out of it.

Strong feelings can happen for a lot of reasons, many of which have nothing to do with being "in love". Maybe you've needed someone, and he has been the one who was there for you. Maybe you're feeling insecure, and he makes you feel beautiful and special. Maybe you've told him all of your deepest, darkest secrets, and that has created a strong feeling of intimacy between you. Maybe you've had some wonderful times together. Maybe there has been very little love in your life, and you are trying to use him to fill that need for you.

Any of these situations can create strong, intense feelings of attraction. They can cause you to care deeply about someone and to miss him intensely when you try to break up with him. But it is wrong to mistake those intense feelings with being "in love" in the truest sense of the word.

Being in love, as we said, is about the whole picture. It is about *everything* clicking together. It is about someone who is nice to you, someone who is there for you, someone you are compatible with, someone you have fun with, someone who is responsible and trustworthy and loving, and someone you *know* would make a terrific spouse and parent.

Some people think that love is "fate" and that some people are just fated to fall in love with people who don't treat them well or with people who are wrong for them. I disagree. That isn't love. These people may experience feelings that mimic feelings of love, but the real thing is far different and far less painful.

When you are in this situation, it is important to examine your feelings of attachment to this person and try to understand why you are feeling them. Are you afraid to be alone? Are you afraid to let go of whatever security this relationship gave you? What is it about this person? What need did he (or she) fill for you?

The next question is the most important: How can you meet that need in a more constructive way? If you are lonely, how can you alleviate that loneliness without turning to him? Do you have friends or family who could help?

If you don't, where could you make friends? Whatever the need is, find a constructive way to fill it.

In the end, situations like this are about courage. You will never grow and develop into the person God intends you to be until you let go of unhealthy relationships, face your fears and develop healthy ways to give and to receive love.

You will get more practical advice on how to handle situations like this in the upcoming chapters. Stay tuned!

Love or Infatuation?

"What is the difference between love and infatuation?"

Love loves the other exactly as he is. Infatuation loves the image he has built of the other person.

Love is being in love with *someone*. Infatuation is being "in love with love".

Love happens gradually, over time. Infatuation happens quickly.

In love, two people get along *better* as time goes by. In infatuation, fights become more frequent and more severe over time.

In love, friends and family tend to approve. In infatuation, friends and family often disapprove.

Love sees the other as an important part of his world. Infatuation sees the other as his whole world.

Love brings out the best in you. It makes you more organized, more productive and more effective. Infatuation can bring out the worst in you. It can make you less organized, less productive and less your "real" self.

Love is consistent. Infatuation comes and goes.

Love seeks to give. Infatuation seeks to get.[1]

Love at First Sight

"Do you believe in 'love at first sight'?"

No. I believe in attraction at first sight. Whether or not that attraction turns into love can only be determined over the following months and years as the two *really* get to know each other.

Does He Love You?

"How do you know when a guy really loves you?"

You will know he loves you by the way he treats you. Is his primary concern what is best for you? Does he look out for you? Is he considerate of your feelings? Does he allow you the freedom to do what you feel you need to do? Does he encourage you to keep up with your other friends and interests, even if that may mean spending less time with him?

---

[1] Adapted from Ray Short, *Sex, Love or Infatuation* (Minneapolis: Augsburg Publishing House, 1978).

As I said above, one of the most important considerations is how he treats you sexually. Does he respect you? Does he make an effort to avoid tempting situations and to keep his desires under control so that he won't do anything that could hurt you? Does he protect your reputation?

If you find someone like this, you have found a treasure. Of course, you shouldn't marry a person *just* because he has these qualities, but you should *never* marry someone who does not have them.

Love or Just Sexual Attraction?

"If part of love is your sexual attraction, and you really like this girl, how do you know if it is truly love and not just hormones?"

John Paul II says that sexual attraction is a good thing when it is a part of what he calls the "storehouse of virtues". In other words, if you say something like this: "I like the fact that she's pretty, she's smart, she's a good person, she's a lot of fun to be around—and I am also very sexually attracted to her", you have sexual attraction in the right perspective.

Sometimes, however, that sexual attraction can cloud your thinking, especially in the early stages of a relationship. How do you know when your feelings are "real" and when they are hormone-induced?

The answer is simple. Don't act on the sexual attraction. It will be there, and it may be very strong. But you don't have to encourage it. Humans have a wonderful gift—we can channel our sexual energy into nonsexual areas. So instead of giving in to the desire to be sexually intimate, focus your attention and energy on the other areas of the relationship. Get to know her. Learn everything you can about her. Watch how she reacts to different situations. Do nice things for her.

While you are dating her, maintain not only chaste behavior but a chaste attitude as well. Do *not* spend your time away from her fantasizing about the sexual things you wish you could do with her. That will make the sexual part of your attraction stronger without helping you to know her any better. It will cloud your certainty. It will make it infinitely more difficult for you to resist temptation when you are with her. It will create two separate "women"— the real woman and the one in your imagination. It will make it easier to "use" the real one, since you are already "using" the imaginary one. And it will take away from that incredible day when you really do give yourself—to her or to someone else. So, if you must daydream, daydream about doing nice things for her. Daydream about the talks you have had and the ideas and dreams you have shared. Daydream about being chaste.

The more time you spend getting to know someone in the context of a chaste relationship, the clearer your real feelings will become. You will begin to realize either (a) she really is everything you ever wanted; or (b) your physical desire was clouding your perception of her.

It may be a struggle to keep your physical desire under control. That's okay—it is good, in fact. You are not a bad person for having those desires. They are normal. That is the way God made you. But every time you refuse to give in to temptation, you are becoming a stronger, more loving, more chaste person.

In Love—But Not with Your Spouse

"Is it possible to marry someone you love very much and then later realize that there is a person you love more? Does this ever happen?"

Yes, it does. But when you get married, you don't promise, "till death, or until someone I like better comes along". You promise "until death", period.

Every marriage, of course, has peaks and valleys. Even in the best marriage, there can and probably will be temptation. After years of marriage, a husband and wife know each other, flaws and all, extremely well. Another person can seem wonderfully mysterious and exciting. But that is only because that person's flaws are still undiscovered. One of the biggest mistakes a married person can make is to confuse attraction to another person with love or read it as a sign that the marriage is somehow "over". Many, many people have left their marriages to be with some new, exciting person, only to realize a few years down the line that this relationship is no better and that this wonderful new person has as many flaws as the person left behind.

Of course, all of this means that it is very important to make a good marriage decision in the first place. There is a song that says, "It's sad to belong to someone else when the right one comes along." And indeed it would be. That is why you should hold out for the right person in the first place. Don't "settle" for someone because you are afraid of growing old alone or because you want to have a big, beautiful wedding or because you want to have children and you just can't wait any longer.

You know the qualities of a good spouse. Pray that you will find one, and then trust God. Wait for the person He sends, the person who has those qualities. Wait until your heart and your head can both agree on someone. Wait for the love of your life. Then, when the excitement has faded and temptation comes along, you will see it for what it is. And you will be confident that, no matter how green the grass may look on the other side, you already have the "love of your life" right there at home.

Using

"How do you tell a girl you know is using you that you know she is using you?"

How about, "I know you are using me"? This phrase is particularly effective when it is followed up with another —"Good-bye."

If it is possible this person may be using you without being aware of it, you may want to try a subtler approach. Try "when you [insert description of how she's using you here], it makes me feel used." See what she says. If she understands and agrees to stop, you may be okay. If she does not understand, reread the previous paragraph.

7

Healing the Hurt

Chastity and Virginity

"What is the difference between chastity and virginity?"

This is an extremely important question. Chastity and virginity are *not* the same thing.

"Virginity" is a technical term. It refers to someone who has never had sex. It is about the past. "Chastity", on the other hand, refers to someone who is living a life of respect for the gift of sexuality *now*, regardless of the mistakes of the past. Chastity is about the present and the future.

When I was in high school, there was a lot of interest in who was a virgin and who was not. That attitude always bothered me. *Why* isn't she a virgin? Was she raped or coerced when she was vulnerable? Did she not realize it was wrong or how it could hurt her? What is her attitude now? Is she trying to live a chaste life? On the other hand, why is someone else a virgin? Is it because she is waiting for marriage, or is she just looking for the right opportunity?

I do *not* want to downgrade virginity. It is extremely beautiful. Those of you who are virgins, please continue to protect your virginity. There are a lot of nonvirgins out there who would give anything to be back in your shoes again. But for those of you who are not virgins, please don't give up. The benefits of chastity are for everyone, and that includes you.

It is nobody's business who is a virgin and who is not. Whatever happened is in the past, and it should stay there. No one can change the past. But the future is wide open. You will determine what it will look like.

"Are you a virgin?"

I am always astounded that so many audiences ask me that question, less than five minutes after I've told them that I don't believe it is anyone's business who is a virgin and who isn't. I don't answer this question for one simple reason: If it is your business whether or not I am a virgin, then it becomes my business whether or not you are virgin. As I said, I don't believe that is any of my business.

I will tell you this much. I live chastity. I am single, I date, and I am saving sex for marriage. I am not asking anything of you that I don't expect of myself as well.

I *do* practice what I preach.

Sin and Forgiveness

"Is premarital sex a really bad sin?"

Most single Christians have heard that premarital sex is a "sin". Unfortunately, many of them have never been taught *why* it is a sin or even what exactly sin *is*.

Yes, the Church teaches that sex outside of a marital relationship is a sin—a serious sin. What does this mean? When I was young, I thought it meant that God was a big Meanie, waiting for us to make mistakes so that he could "doom us to hell". This was difficult for me to understand —that image just didn't square with "The loving God" that we made collages and wrote poems about in CCD class.

We need to start by understanding sin. Sin isn't just a matter of breaking some abstract rule that God made up to torture us. God created us. He knows how we operate. Morality is not abstract. Moral laws are simply the instruction manual for living our lives. To sin means to go against the way we are made. To sin is in some way to hurt others and ourselves. God hates to see that.

We have seen how this applies to sexuality. God created sex to speak a beautiful language—the language of permanent, committed, fruitful marital love. When we try to take sex out of that context, it doesn't work, and we get hurt—physically, emotionally and spiritually.

But sin goes beyond just "bumming God out" or making Him sad because we are hurting ourselves or each other. We were made for God, and living according to the way we were made brings us closer to Him. Going against the way we were made, on the other hand, takes us farther away from Him. When we deliberately sin, we say to God, "I know you want me to do it this way, but I don't care. I am going to do it my way." There are consequences for that kind of attitude. When we deliberately, knowingly commit a serious sin, we cut ourselves off from God and from His graces. That is a very bad position to be in, especially if you happen to die. When you die, He is all that is left. To be cut off from Him at that point is, literally, hell.

Deliberate sin cuts us off from God. Who is doing the cutting? Big mean God? No. We are. When we sin, we are making our own decisions. We do the cutting. God doesn't like it. He is madly in love with each and every one of us. He wants us to be with Him. He wants us to come back.

This is true for all sins, including sexual sins. Yes, deliberately abusing the gift of sexuality is a serious sin. Left unrepented, this sin cuts us off from God. He, however, doesn't want things to stay this way. He doesn't want us to separate ourselves from Him. He still loves us madly. He wants us back.

Move on to the next question to learn how to make that happen.

"Does God forgive people who have sex?"

"If you've already had sex, are you doomed to hell?"

Most people growing up today haven't heard the truth about chastity. Most of them don't understand the beauty of God's gift of sexuality. Many people get more information about sex from MTV than they do from their Church. Is it any surprise, then, that so many single Christians are engaging in sexual activity? Of course not.

What happens then, when these people learn about chastity? What happens when they find out that this sexual activity was wrong and that it hurt them? Is God up there saying, "Ha! You sinned!! Now I can nail you!!!"

Wrong, wrong, *wrong*. God loves us. He doesn't love us more when we are being good and less when we are being bad. It grieves Him to see us turn away from Him. He wants us to turn back.

As Catholics, we have a tremendous gift—the sacrament of confession. There we can go directly to God and make things right again. All He asks of us is that we be *truly* sorry and to resolve to try not to commit that sin again. He pumps us full of grace, and we are back in business.

There's a beautiful scene in the movie *Jesus of Nazareth*. Jesus is having dinner with the Pharisees. This is a big deal—it would be like one of us eating at an embassy or the governor's mansion or someplace important like that. While they are eating, they are having a discussion about the command to "love your neighbor". Just as Joseph of Arimathea asks "But who is my neighbor?", Mary Magdalen bursts into the room. Mary Magdalen is not a Pharisee, and she is not someone you would expect to see in a Pharisee's house. She is, as depicted in the movie, a prostitute. She is screaming to see Jesus, and everyone is calling her names and trying to drag her out of the room. But Jesus says, "Let her stay." She falls at Jesus' feet, weeping. She knows she has sinned, and she bitterly regrets it. Jesus looks at her with an absolutely incredible look of love and says, "Your sins, and I know they are many, are forgiven you because of your great love. Go, and sin no more."

Rent that movie some time, and watch that scene. Look at the expression of love on His face. That is the way He looks at you in the sacrament of confession. That is how deeply and tenderly He loves you.

The confessional is very important to us as Catholics. It brings us to a priest who was given Christ's own authority to forgive sins (Jn 20:22–23). Confession allows us to hear those beautiful words, "I absolve you from your sins . . ." with our own ears. It gives us a guarantee of forgiveness. Most importantly, the sacrament gives us grace—strength and help from God so that we can live up to the promise to "go and sin no more."

Please don't be afraid of the confessional. You cannot possibly "shock" the priest. He listens to people's sins all the time—he has heard it all before. If you don't want the priest to know who you are, that is okay. You don't have to go "face to face" if you're not comfortable with it— you can stay behind the screen. It is good, however, always to go to the same priest each time if possible, so that he knows a little about your past, even if he doesn't know your name. Then he can better advise you on what to do in the future. Better yet, have a priest whom you know and who knows you. It is best if you find one who is very holy and who understands and is enthusiastic about the new chastity movement among Catholic singles. Talk to him on a regular basis. Ask him for help in living chastity. Again, don't worry about shocking him or telling him "secrets". You cannot shock him, and the Church says he cannot reveal what he heard in the confessional, even if his life is threatened. He would die before divulging your secrets. The confessional is there for you. Use it regularly. Don't "spin your wheels" wondering if something you did is wrong. Don't just wallow in guilt. Get the link back up, and start fresh.

"What if you commit a bad sin, but you didn't know it was a sin when you were doing it?"

God is not some big bad guy up in heaven waiting for us to blow it so that He can nail us. He is absolute justice but also absolute love.

In order to be personally responsible for a sin, you have to make a *decision* to disobey God. It is not possible to cut yourself off "accidentally" from God. Now don't get me wrong—if you commit a sin without fully understanding what you're doing, a bad thing has still happened. Sin is damage, and the damage will happen regardless of what you knew or didn't know. The physical and emotional consequences will happen regardless of what you knew or did not know. But in order to be spiritually responsible, you have to choose freely to sin, and to understand that what you are doing is a sin.

But, on the other hand, you have an obligation to learn about the faith, and that includes learning about sin. If you keep "unknowingly" sinning because you never bother learning what God expects of His followers, expect to do a lot of explaining on Judgment Day.

What if you had premarital sex, but you didn't realize it was a sin at the time? It was a bad idea, obviously. It put you at serious physical and emotional risk. But did you cut yourself off from God?

God is the judge of these things—not you or I. Don't just sit around worrying about it or panicking. Go to the priest in the confessional and ask him. Explain the situation, ask him to absolve you from any sin you may have committed, and commit to making every effort to live chastity in the future. Then thank God for His amazing, incredible love, and look forward to your new life of chastity!

"If you confess to a sin during confession and then commit that sin again, is it worse than the first time?"

When you confess a sin, you are saying that you're sorry it ever happened and that you are going to try very, very hard to keep it from happening again.

If at some point in the future you are weak, and you commit that sin again, go back into the confessional and confess it again. It's okay to do that. We are weak human beings, and despite our best efforts, we sometimes sin again. That original sin problem tends to keep cropping up.

Please, don't *ever* stop going to confession. Don't ever figure "I've confessed this sin too many times. I give up." As long as you're trying to stop, God keeps forgiving—as many times as it takes.

"I went to confession, but I don't feel forgiven. I still think a lot about what I did, and I feel really bad about it."

Even though you have been forgiven, you may not always "feel" forgiven. It is very tempting for people who have committed sexual sin to say, "Oh, I'm a bad person. If those other Christians knew the bad thing I did, they wouldn't like me anymore. How can God forgive me for doing something so terrible?"

Nothing is deadlier for someone who has confessed a sin than to waste all his energy thinking "I'm such a bad person." We are all bad people—or at least good people with bad tendencies. That is why we have confession. When we make a mistake, we need to confess it and *move on.*

If you have made a mistake in the past, it is important to think about it to a certain extent. Only, however, because you need to understand *why* it happened, so that you don't let it happen again. You need to know what situations to avoid and how to make sure there's plenty of positive love in your life. Beyond that, there is no need to dwell on the past.

A confessed sin is *gone*; God has taken it away and forgotten about it. He loves you immensely, and He is only interested in your future. But how can you concentrate on your future if you're stuck in the past, beating yourself over the head because you sinned? That is not God working in you. It is Satan, trying to tempt you by focusing your attention on something God has already forgotten. He is trying to make you feel unworthy and to lower your self-esteem, so that you will fall again. Don't fall for it.

Don't expect to *feel* forgiven right away or suddenly to forget your sin. It doesn't necessarily work that way. Just keep reminding yourself that you *are* forgiven, whether you feel it or not. Christ Himself told you so.

The key to all of this is that God loves you. Remember that, stay close to Him, and concentrate on building a positive future. With His help, anything is possible. Even starting over! So look to God, look ahead and go for it.

"If you were raped or something, would you still be considered a virgin even though you were forced?"

"Is it a sin when someone in your family molests you?"

"My friend was raped. Is she a sinner?"

"I've been sexually abused by my dad. Am I impure?"

All real questions. I hear many more like them.

If someone is raped or sexually abused, she has not sinned. She is a victim. The person who did this to her has sinned—badly. But she is not responsible.

In addition, if this is the only sexual experience she has ever had, she is still, in a very real sense, a virgin. Virginity is a gift—it must be given away. It cannot be violently taken.

If you or someone you know has been raped or sexually abused, get help *immediately*. Talk to a priest, parent or school counselor, or call one of the numbers in Appendix 2 in the back of this book.

"If nonvirgins can just start over, why shouldn't I just go out and lose my virginity and then 'repent'? Then I can have the best of both worlds."

Wrong. You will not get the best of both worlds. Anyone who has repented and started over will confirm this. You will risk serious physical and emotional consequences that can be difficult to overcome. And I can almost guarantee that the sex will not be that great.

In addition, you will be trying to "put one over" on God, which does not work. To repent means to be sorry about something. It means to regret ever doing it. You cannot "plan" to repent for something you are still intending to do.

Virgins, don't take your virginity lightly. It is a beautiful gift—treasure it.

Starting Over

"Can one not be a virgin yet change and be whole again?"

I chose to include this particular question because I thought her phrasing was very insightful. "Whole." I had not used that word in my talk that day, but she had obviously experienced the lack of "wholeness" that comes from losing virginity in the wrong context.

Loss of virginity in an unmarried relationship is often a surprisingly traumatic experience. Instead of the euphoric glow of "sexual maturity", many find themselves feeling alone, empty and strangely "different". Fear of pregnancy or diseases often compounds that trauma. Relationships, instead of improving, often deteriorate. Self-esteem often takes a serious nose-dive.

Yet, often there is a reluctance to link sex with this subsequent misery. "It must be me. It is never like this on TV. A couple more times and I'll be fine. I can't stop now or I'll lose him for sure."

Only a couple more times, and it still isn't fine. What you were going through was not just your own neurosis, and it was not just "adjustment". It was your psyche, your emotions and your soul, all crying out, "Don't do this. We weren't made for this, You're cutting us off from God." And if you feel "better" after a few more times, it just means that you have buried those "warnings" a little deeper into your subconscious.

But buried feelings are not very good at staying in the subconscious. They come back in little ways. Resentment can develop between you and your "partner". Tension often develops with your family. You may feel resentment toward people you classify as "good". You may feel profoundly uncomfortable around God.

Is the solution to pop the Pill and try to have some fun? I think not. Potential pregnancy and disease, as disastrous as they could be, are actually among the least of your problems. You have (often unknowingly) gone against the way you were made. You have cut yourself off from God. That does serious damage to your "self-esteem" and to your sense of identity as someone created in the image and likeness of God. This phenomenon is called "guilt", and it serves as a warning that you are hurting yourself and often someone else. The solution is not to ignore the guilt but rather to deal with the underlying cause.

In the course of my travels, I have met, prayed with and cried with more women than I could count; women who did not expect it to be this way. They thought sex was what they were supposed to do. They thought that sex was the "adult" way to show love. They thought it would be great. They thought sex would make them happy. But it wasn't, it wasn't, it wasn't, and it didn't.

Every time I meet someone like this, I get a little angry. I am angry for them. I am angry that they had to learn this one the hard way. I am angry that so many of their teachers and role models are copping out on them. I am angry that so few people are willing to acknowledge what these people are experiencing and to help them through it. I am angry that so few people, even in the churches, offer these people concrete ways for getting back on track.

Yes, you can be "whole" again. I will do everything I can to show you how.

"Can I live chastity even if I am not a virgin?"

Yes, you can!!! Anyone who comes to understand the beauty and the meaning of sexuality can make a commitment to live chastity, regardless of the past.

The world seems to have a skewed attitude toward sexual activity. People say that once you have started, you are not going to be able to stop. Statistics classify teenagers who have only done it once as "sexually active", even though many of those do not return to sexual activity. Sex-education instructors are often told to emphasize abstinence for teens who have not had sexual relationships and birth control for those who have.

Funny, they don't have that attitude about anything else. No one says, "Well, now that you have tried drugs, I guess you will keep it up. Here is a roach clip—don't burn your fingers." Or, "Gee, you got drunk. I guess we will never see you sober at a party again." People are constantly being urged not to repeat their past mistakes—except when it comes to sex.

A lot of people tend to think that, once they have lost their virginity, they are somehow "tainted" forever. Word might be out among their friends. They feel they have joined a different "club", and there is no going back. Their sex-education classes tell them that they had better start looking into birth control. They are uneasy about church and wary of God. It becomes easy to drift away from Him.

It is all so unnecessary. There is hope. You can join literally millions of others across the country and around the world who are returning to lives of chastity after realizing that sexual activity was hurting their lives.

If they can do it, you can.

"I want to start over, but you said that chastity doesn't happen automatically. What steps should I take to insure I don't mess up again?"

In the next chapter, we will talk about some general guidelines for *anyone* who wants to live chastity. Here, however, I want to give some guidelines specifically for those of you who are starting over.

1. *Go to confession:* This goes without saying. The first step to making your life right again is making your relationship with God right again. There are all kinds of graces attached to confession that will make the next steps easier.

2. *Pray:* Once you have restored your relationship with God, it is important to continue that relationship. Pray regularly. Attend Mass. Receive communion. Stay close to God. Ask Him for the help you will constantly need to live a life of chastity.

Along these lines, you should make a special effort to make the Eucharist a part of your life. Jesus said, "Unless you eat the flesh of the Son of Man and drink his blood, you have no life in you" (Jn 6:23). How much sexual activity is a result of feeling that we have no life in us? The Eucharist is Jesus—body, blood, soul and divinity. It is the whole Jesus, the One who loves you more than anyone, physically present right in front of you. He fills you with His love. There is tremendous supernatural power in the Eucharist.

Try to make the Eucharist a part of your daily life. Receive communion every day. Spend time praying in front of the Blessed Sacrament. Find a church in your area with perpetual adoration (where the Eucharist is displayed in the church or chapel for worship and adoration). If you can't find perpetual adoration, just go to your own church where He is present in the tabernacle. Spend a half-hour a day, or fifteen minutes a day, or an hour a week, or whatever, in His presence. Pray the rosary, pray in your own words or just sit there and absorb His love. Ask Him to give you His Love. Ask Him to take charge of your future.

Even if it doesn't feel spiritually moving at the time, I guarantee that if you stick with it, this can be a life-changing experience. Over time, it will help you heal your pain.

3. *Have a buddy system:* When you are starting over, or just trying to resist temptation, it is tough to struggle alone. Obviously, you need God's help, which comes through prayer. But it is also good to have a youth leader or a priest or someone who believes what you believe and who is willing to help you to live chastity. You should talk to this person every time you go on a date or even go anywhere with someone you are attracted to. You should tell him in advance what your plans are. Being more objective, this person can say, "Hey, you promised you'd never be alone with him in his house again." You should also talk to this person *after* every date, so that you can go over what went right (or wrong). Knowing you are going to do this can be pretty helpful in the heat of temptation. If you slip up again, you will be accountable to someone. That can help you to stop.

4. *Fill your life with positive love:* We have talked about how many teenagers get involved in sexual activity because they are trying to find the real love that is missing in their lives. Trying to find that love in sex doesn't work. But neither does trying to eliminate sex without dealing with the root of the problem. Humans do not need sex, but we do need love.

What should we do when our lives lack love? Sometimes we can't do much about absent parents or problems in our families. We can't help it if the people around us are not very loving. But there is one person you can control—

yourself. You can *be* a loving person. That makes a difference. With love, what goes around, comes around.

Make an effort to fill your life with love for the people around you. Volunteer some place where people need you—a soup kitchen, a CCD program, nursing home visitation, whatever. When you spend your time spreading Christ's love, it is amazing how little time you have left to be tempted by counterfeits.

5. *Develop your talents:* Unchaste behavior feeds on low self-esteem. If you don't like yourself, it is more difficult to respect your sexuality. Making mistakes sexually, conversely, causes even lower self-esteem. You can stop that vicious cycle by learning to see your incredible dignity in God's eyes.

God put each of us here for a reason. We each have a role to play in His plan. To help us achieve that role, He gave us each gifts. That includes you. You have gifts and talents. Maybe you're good at singing or sports or painting or something else. Whatever you are good at, it's important for you to find those gifts and to develop them. They will give you an outlet for your energy, help you to develop self-discipline and help you to find your own place in God's plan.

6. *Know your limits:* If you have been sexually active before, those limits will be different from what they will be for someone who has never had sex.

You have probably formed certain habits, and that means you need to be even more vigilant.

If being in a certain dark room used to lead to sex, the best thing to do is to avoid that dark room. If certain types of affection used to lead to sex, the best thing to do is to find other forms of affection instead. The old maxim has never been more true: Know thyself. And do not overestimate thine own strength.

Healing the Hurt

"What is a good way to get over a sexual relationship? I've already stopped thinking about everything, but I can't stop thinking about the person. That person has totally forgotten about me. I thought we could remain friends, but it's not working out. Please help me."

"I loved her and resisted so long, but I finally gave in and the result was so much pain. After giving myself to the girl I loved, I was so hurt to find rejection."

"I had sex with a guy I really liked and I fell in love with him. Now he doesn't talk to me. I can't get over him. It's been two years now."

This is only a small sample of the literally hundreds of teens and single adults who have shared with me the seemingly unending pain they are enduring as a result of the breakup of a sexual relationship.

To all of you I say the same thing: You are not alone. I know that may mean very little right now; your pain is your pain, and it is much more real to you than the hypothetical pain of some guy in Cleveland or a girl in Tulsa. But believe me, it is true. You are not alone.

I want more than anything to "make it better"—for you and for anyone who has experienced this kind of pain and disappointment.

The breakup of a sexual relationship is painful, obviously, because that immensely strong emotional bond has been broken. You have given yourself completely, and now you feel rejected completely. Even if it is not logical, even if *you are the one who did the breaking up*, that pain is often immense.

The good news is that there *is* healing. Time heals all wounds. And by working with God and following some simple steps, you can often speed up that process considerably. Some of those steps I discussed in the last question, but I want to repeat them for you.

The thing to do in this situation, painful as it may seem, is to get on with your life. Do something good for yourself. Develop your talents. Throw yourself into improving your life. Do what you're good at, so you can *see* God's beautiful work in your life. As you watch yourself improve at something, your self-esteem will grow.

If you were relying on this relationship to fill your need for love, you are probably experiencing a serious void in that area of your life right now. In a way, this can be good. This pain is like an alarm telling you that something was wrong. This is a way of learning that sex was not and is not the way to find that kind of real love.

The right way to fill that need is to go out and live love. Concentrate on the people around you. Take a look at your friends and family. Have you appreciated them? Have you loved them the way you should, or have you been so wrapped up in your pain that you have not even noticed them lately? Spend some time really building healthy relationships with the people who are important to you. Good, solid, loving families and friendships can give you a base of support and keep you from "needing" your dates to fill your need to give and receive love.

Then take that love outside. Do something for the community. Volunteer in a soup kitchen, a homeless shelter or a day-care center. Helping someone else is the best way to change your perspective about yourself and about love.

The wrong way to deal with this hurt is by trying to reconcile with the person who hurt you. When you broke up, you felt totally rejected. You may still feel totally rejected. It is very tempting, after being "rejected" like this, to tie all of your self-esteem up with the person who rejected you. You say, "I feel bad about myself because he rejected me, and the only way for me to feel good about myself again is to make him love me again." This is very dangerous. Repeat: *This is very dangerous.* This kind of thinking is probably the leading cause of mismatched couples reconciling six, seven or eight times and making themselves and each other miserable over and over again.

Another wrong way to fill that need is to go out right away and get another boyfriend or girlfriend. This is known as the "rebound", and it is a serious mistake. It amounts to using another person the way you were using the last person. It keeps you in this unhealthy cycle, even if you manage to avoid sex in the new relationship. You still haven't dealt with the root issue.

If you just got out of a painful relationship, you may

not even be particularly interested in anyone else. A lot of people say to me, "I can't give her up. There's no one else I want." It is perfectly normal and healthy not to want anyone else right away. For all of the pain in your last relationship, you probably knew each other very well and shared a great deal of intimacy. Someone new is a "blank slate", and that will not be as attractive to you right now.

Give yourself time to heal. Concentrate on building strong relationships with your family, your friends and God. Do not start dating again until you have done that.

Most importantly, be patient. You may be feeling very empty and "dark", and those feelings may not go away immediately, even if you are doing everything right. The thing to do is to say, "Okay, dark feelings, so you're here with me again today. Well, I have a busy day. You're welcome to come along if you'd like, but bear in mind that I plan to ignore you."

Then do it. Don't worry about your dark feelings, become obsessed about them or try to "make" them go away. Just acknowledge that they exist, but don't dwell on them. Spend your energy building the best life possible for yourself. Then, eventually, I assure you—those feelings will go away.

Healing the Relationship

"How can you move from a sexual relationship to a nonsexual relationship?"

"How do you rekindle relationships that have been destroyed by sexual activity?"

The first question to ask is not "How?"; it is "Should I?".

If you realize that your relationship is going badly, and you believe that sex is the reason, the first step is to *stop sexual activity*. No ifs, ands or buts. Sex creates a strong bond that distorts your true feelings for each other. You need to cease all sexually arousing affection before you can determine how you feel about each other or repair any damage sexual activity has done to your relationship.

Stopping sexual activity is much easier said than done. We have talked about some of the difficulties for an individual in starting over. A couple who have had sex will have a far *more* difficult time stopping while remaining together. I am not saying that it can't be done—just that you need to be *very* vigilant. Habits have formed, and you need to be extremely aware of them so that you can avoid tempting situations.

After you have abstained for a while, see how things go. Are you able to restrain yourselves sexually out of love for each other? Are you getting along better? Do you recognize now that your sexual activity was hurting you and your relationship?

If the answer is "yes", and you've been able to work through your problems, then move forward cautiously. You may have accomplished something very significant, but you still need plenty of time to be certain.

If the answer is "no"—if you haven't been able to work out your problems, or if you keep falling back into sexual sin—then it is time to end the relationship. Don't drag your feet once you realize this. Sticking around in a damaged relationship will only make things worse.

Can We Be Friends?

"I had a sexual relationship that ended badly. How do I put everything in the past and become friends again?"

"Becoming friends again" is much easier said than done. I believe that it is *extremely* difficult to maintain a friendship with someone with whom you have had sex, especially if it "ended badly".

There is significant pain in the breakup of a sexual relationship. That person's continuing presence in your life can be a constant reminder of that pain. It can keep you from healing.

I speak to so many single people who tell me, "I promised we'd always be friends." They say they are staying in this person's life because they want to keep that promise, but I believe the real reason goes deeper. They don't want to "let go" all the way. They want to hang on to some of the intimacy and security they got from the other person.

Either way, this is a serious mistake. "We will always be friends" is a promise that often cannot be kept. The emotional toll is way too high. And trying to use that promise in order to hold on to the intimacy or the security of the relationship doesn't work. It just keeps you imprisoned longer.

When you break off a sexual relationship, you need a clean break. You *absolutely* need a certain period of time where you don't see the other person—a time for you to heal and to rebuild your own life. Trying to forge a "friendship" at this point will only disturb the process of rebuilding your life.

Maybe in time you can be friends. Maybe. But for now, don't expect anything, and don't rush anything. Take some time to rebuild your own life—on your own.

"I really want to stay friends with my ex. He hasn't come back to the Church yet, but sometimes he seems like he's on his way. He also relies on me emotionally. I want to be there to help him, but it's so painful. I'm sure the fact that we had sex doesn't help. Can there be peace in not communicating with someone I love so much and want to help?"

Believe me, I am more than sympathetic to your situation. I have been in a similar situation, and I know the pain. Situations like this are difficult no matter what, and yours is further complicated by the presence of a shared sexual history.

You are not God, and you are not Superwoman. You can't *make* him love God. He has all of the information.

There is nothing more you can tell him. You can't "save" him. That is up to him.

But you need to save *you*. You need some peace in your life.

I can't tell you what to do, but I think you have answered your own question. There can be peace in not communicating with him. I honestly believe it is the only peace you will find right now. All of this turmoil means that the bond is still present and still very, very strong. It is not going to go away as long as he is a presence in your life.

Think about the times you have been away from him for a while—the times you met new people or did new things or started getting on with your life. There was peace, wasn't there? I'll bet you felt great. But then he came back, and you thought you were strong enough this time and that you could be his friend and help him. But then the peace went away. You were sucked in again, and the turmoil started all over, didn't it?

Don't think you have to be at peace and be friends with all of your ex's. That is nonsense. And, as I said in answer to the last question, it is almost impossible to be friends with someone with whom you have had sex, especially if he was your "first". You were just not made that way.

There is a term that is overused in psychological circles today but that is significant here. The term is "co-dependent", and it basically means being addicted to being "needed" by someone else. You seem to be a little bit addicted to the idea that your ex somehow "needs" you. But he doesn't. You are not responsible for his life—he is. If he is going to change, it will be because he chooses to, not because you make him.

I know it feels good to be needed, but you need to be free to find the best possible spouse, so that you can be needed in the right way—by a well-adjusted husband who gives instead of just taking and by children who, as children, will rely on you completely. In the meantime, this situation is preventing you from being free to do that. Even if you are technically free, you are not emotionally free. And I don't believe you will be as long as your ex keeps popping back into your life.

Don't worry about your ex. I am sure he is a big boy, and he can take care of himself. You are doing him no favor by doing things for him. He needs to stand on his own two feet. Don't worry about stupid promises you may have made. Worry about getting on with your life.

"I know my ex isn't good for me, but I keep going back. I know it's because we had sex, and now losing him is just too painful. We try to break up and 'just be friends', but that hurts too. Help!"

I want you to remember something. There are two kinds of pain. The first is bad pain. It is like the pain from an untreated infection or wound. That kind of pain is not getting you anywhere. It just gets worse and worse until you do something about it. The second kind of pain is like the pain you have from working out. It hurts in the short run, but it is getting you somewhere. It is making you stronger. It won't hurt forever.

The pain you are experiencing right now is bad pain. I don't see any resolution. You share a sexual history but no real present compatibility, and your sexual past has done a lot to damage your chances for a platonic present. It just keeps hurting.

If you walk away, it will hurt. I am not denying that. But that pain will be the second kind. It will require courage, for sure. You will need to be strong to resist picking up the phone when you are tempted to call him. But when you resist once, it will be easier the next time. I promise you will get to a point where it won't hurt anymore.

I know it is hard to believe things can get better—but they can. I promise.

"I Got Drunk"

"I have always practiced chastity. However, not long ago I got drunk and went very far with a guy. It seems like something that happened in a different world and that it wasn't me that did something so stupid. I've cried a lot over this. Do you think that even though I didn't have intercourse I still lost my virginity? Can't I just accept God's forgiveness and move on?"

First of all, you know God forgives you. Through the sacrament of reconciliation, in the confessional, God takes your sin *away*. (If you haven't been to confession yet—*go!*) Now there are two things left for you to do—understand and accept that forgiveness, and understand what happened, so you can be sure it never happens again.

171

To answer your questions about what happened. First of all, you did not lose your virginity. That means having intercourse, which you did not do. And, on a more significant level, virginity is something that has to be given away freely. You were drunk, and with a guy you didn't even know. You were significantly out of control, and my guess is that you were taken advantage of by this guy.

Getting drunk is a sneaky thing. What it does, as you have found, is shut your brain down. It takes away that part of your brain that says, "I shouldn't do this", and it just leaves the part that says, "That feels good." Or "I don't feel anything, but I don't seem to be able to stop." And, more importantly, it takes away your "startle" reflex. As someone who has practiced chastity, you probably tend to jump back when someone does something to you that he should not do. That reflex is gone when you are drunk. The tendency then is to think, "This shouldn't be happening, but I can't seem to do anything about it, so I'll just keep going."

You said "it wasn't me that did something so stupid." In a sense, you are right. It wasn't you. When you are drunk, you are not yourself, or at least not your whole self. You were not a terrible, horrible person. You were a drunk person, and you did what drunk people are inclined to do. That is how drunk people are often used by other people, especially selfish people like that guy.

Please stop being so hard on yourself. The fact that this happened does not mean you are not a good, strong, chaste person who believes in respecting sex. It means that you got drunk, and that can erase even the strongest intentions. God can work good out of these things for us by remind-

172

ing us that we are weak. We are all weak, not just you. I am weak, your friends are weak, our parents are weak. We are all affected by original sin, and we should never be too confident that we can avoid sin on our own. We need to be vigilant, and we need God's help.

If you don't want this to happen again (which I know you don't), you cannot get drunk anymore. Your biggest sin that night was not what happened to you. You had very little control over that. Your main sin was in letting yourself get to a point where you were not able to protect yourself or your gift of sexuality. Don't fool yourself into thinking that "next time I'll be smarter." Next time you will be exactly the same if you are drunk again. That is how you operate with part of your brain shut down. It is how that weakness we all have gets hold of you.

You were lucky this time. I can't tell you how many girls just like you I've talked to—girls who were waiting for marriage, got drunk and got *pregnant* by guys they didn't know. Talk about a bad situation! Please, please make and keep a commitment to stick with Pepsi at parties for now. And find friends who will do it, too, and help you do it. If you find that you *can't* stop drinking, check into Alcoholics Anonymous or a similar twelve-step program. You absolutely *need* to stop drinking. It is the only way you can be sure of protecting that very beautiful gift of sexuality.

Finally, do not keep dwelling on this. Just remember that God loves you and forgives you, that you're not a horrible, awful person, just a weak one like everyone else. You let the weakness get ahead of you, but you are going to work hard not to let it happen again. Satan loves nothing more than to keep whispering in our ears, "You did a bad thing. You are a bad person now. You are different from those other Christians." Don't let it work. You were created in the image and likeness of God, and you are just like those other Christians. And remember—you are redeemed!! Christ knew that you were weak, and He died for you, for that weakness. That is why St. Paul gloried in his weakness. Christ loves you with a tender, all-encompassing love. He loves you now more than ever. Hold fast to that, and hold fast to Him. You will be fine.

Unforgiving Friends

"I've always been committed to living chastity, but recently I made a mistake. I want to start over, but my friends who are still virgins are ignoring me now."

People who never seem to sin are sometimes the ones who sin the most. They can be tempted to look down their noses at everyone else, saying, "I've never committed a sexual sin and you have, so I'm better than you." That is pride, and it is a lot bigger sin than what happened to you. Maybe if this had not happened to you, you would be tempted to act like that, too. This will make you a whole lot more understanding toward others when they are weak, won't it? You have been there. As a result of what you are going through now, you will be better able to help others.

Repent, pray, get on with your life, and do not dwell on the past. God can write straight with crooked lines—let Him do it for you.

Let this also serve as a warning to you virgins out there, and to anyone else who feels "above" anyone who sins. Virginity is a gift. You are very blessed to have had whatever background, training and graces you have received that have allowed you to protect that gift. But remember that key word—blessed. Others may not have had the background, training or graces you have received. And you have no idea how well you would fare in another's shoes. Don't judge—it's not your job. Reach out in friendship and love. That is your job—your only job.

Sex is not the biggest sin. Pride is. Be careful.

"He Had Sex with Someone Else"

"Last year my boyfriend and I broke up for a couple of months and then got back together. Now I've found out that while we were apart, he had sex with another girl. He says he still loves me and that it didn't mean anything. I know I have no right to be upset because he had no obligation to me at the time, but I can't get it out of my mind."

You have every right to be upset. Sex speaks the language of forever, of permanent commitment. You are not wired to "share" someone you love sexually. The thought of someone you love having sex with someone else should be absolutely, horrifyingly repugnant to you. To accept that someone loved you while having sex with someone else goes against every protective mechanism you have.

He may not have had a formal obligation to you. But he did and does have an obligation to himself, to that girl and to whatever woman he may marry in the future. And, in doing what he did, he violated every single one of those obligations. He sinned against God. He used his body to tell that woman a lie—the lie that he was giving himself to her forever. He put her at significant physical, emotional and spiritual risk. He cheated on his future wife, if he is to have one.

Do not try to convince yourself that this is all right. Do not try to stifle the voice that tells you something is wrong here. It is not all right. There is definitely something wrong.

What is his attitude now? Does he understand chastity? Does he fully recognize what a horrible thing he did? Is he truly repentant? Most importantly, is he strong enough to live chastity in the future?

If the answer to any of these questions is "no", it would probably be a good idea to get out. Don't try to use his "commitment" to you as a way to force him to live chastity. He needs to live chastity for himself, out of his *own* belief in the value and dignity of sexuality. If he doesn't believe in that value and dignity, or if he sees nothing wrong with having sex with someone to whom he is not married and about whom he does not even care, he is not the kind of man you could trust as a husband. If *you* and your beliefs are his only motivation, his resolve will fade eventually— probably soon. How could you ever fully trust him?

Sex and Your Future Spouse

"I've made mistakes in my past, but now I'm committed to living chastity. But if I get married, will I have to tell my husband about my mistakes?"

That depends on whom you marry. Some people may think it is important to know things like that, others may not. But the important thing is that, if you have lived chastity since you made the commitment to do so, you have in a sense "saved yourself" during that time. That is a gift.

When you first commit a sexual sin, the memory looms large, and you can't imagine telling someone else about it. But time will help to heal, and someone who loves you and who sees your commitment to chastity should not reject you for the mistakes in your past.

"Why should I save myself for marriage if my future husband hasn't saved himself?"

Why indeed?

One good thing about living chastity is that it tends to raise your standards for a spouse. Why save yourself all those years just to give yourself to someone who doesn't understand the value of that gift? Why give it to someone who has nothing to give back?

None of this means that you have to marry a virgin. What is important is not whether or not your future husband is a virgin. If God can forgive mistakes in the past, you can too. The important questions are these: What is his attitude *now*? Does he understand chastity? Has he been "saving himself" since he came to understand chastity? Does he live it? Has he proven that he has the strength and self-control necessary to live chastity? Has he been able to live it for a significant period of time? Has he proven that he can be trusted after you are married? If the answer is "yes", he sounds like a pretty great guy.

Whether you and your spouse tell each other about your "sexual history" is up to you. But one thing is important. If you are not absolutely certain that this person is a virgin, insist on comprehensive sexually transmitted disease testing before the wedding. Some very contagious diseases can lie dormant for years without ever causing any symptoms. God always forgives, but nature doesn't necessarily follow suit.

"I Can't Stop"

"Why is it so difficult to live chastity sometimes? I know it's the right thing to do, but sometimes it's a real struggle anyway."

"What does original sin have to do with sex?"

We all see some kind of gap between conviction and action somewhere in our lives, whether in eating, exercise, prayer or whatever. We know what we should do, but we don't always do it. The good news is that we are in good company. In his letter to the Romans, St. Paul said, "I cannot understand my own behavior. I fail to carry out the things I want to do, and I find myself doing the very things I hate" (Rom 7:15). So, if a guy as holy as St. Paul had to deal with this problem, it must be universal.

What is the problem? As St. Paul goes on to say, "When I act against my own will, then, it is not my true self doing it, but the sin which lives in me" (Rom 7:17). This is because we are all affected by original sin—we are inclined to do things we know are not good for us. There is a constant battle between good and evil going on inside of us.

So what is the answer? "Oh, well, sin lives in me, so I guess I can't fight it. I'll use a condom and everything will be fine." Wrong. Especially with a gift as beautiful as sexuality, we are called to struggle *against* our sinful nature, to live up to our dignity.

When it comes to sex, this can be difficult. First of all, the human sexual urge is very strong. Once we get tempted, we are *really* tempted. There is a reason for that. Our bodies are made to move forward, toward intercourse. If they were not made that way, people would be satisfied just making out all the time, and the world would never be repopulated. But once you get the engine rolling, it is a lot more difficult to stop. Your brain shuts off. So anyone who tries to be chaste but doesn't avoid those tempting situations is going to have a problem. This is especially true for people who have done it and are trying to start over. Habits are formed, and it is very easy for one thing to lead to another when that is where they have always gone before.

There are deeper reasons for repeated failure of sexual self-control. We have talked about how many unmarried people are involved in sexual activity because they are looking for love. The ones who have experienced the least love in their lives are the ones who are most likely to be involved in sexual activity, and they are the ones who have the most difficult time quitting. And it is no wonder. If you are one of these, and you try to quit without dealing with the lack of love in your life, you will still be tempted (often subconsciously) to seek counterfeit love in sexual activity. You are trying to fill a void that still exists in your life—a void sex cannot fill. But that void makes the temptation much more powerful. You need to fill that void—with real love.

No matter how hard you try to live chastity, you are almost bound for failure if you don't base your efforts on prayer. The tendency toward sin in us is very strong, and we need God's grace and His help if we are going to succeed. Chastity is like a muscle. When you first lift a weight, it can feel very heavy. But the stronger the muscle gets, the easier it is to lift the weight. And if the Holy Spirit is behind you holding the bar, lifting the weight is a *whole* lot easier. That strength comes through prayer.

"I really want to live chastity. I've tried to stop having sex, but I must be too weak or something. I just keep going back. I'm starting to feel really bad about myself."

You may be unsuccessful at living chastity because you are not fueling your efforts with a lot of prayer. Maybe you are failing because you are not avoiding tempting situations. Or maybe you are subconsciously looking for love.

There is another possible explanation. You may be suffering from some form of sexual or relationship addiction. I will discuss those in the next questions.

Sexual Addiction

"Define 'sexual addiction'."

"Sexual addiction" does not just refer to someone who enjoys sex or someone who goes too far on a date. A sexual addict is someone for whom the sex drive has become seriously out of control. The sex addict is controlled by sex, much as an alcoholic is controlled by booze.

Like other addicts, a sexual addict will risk everything—career, marriage, reputation—for a "fix" of sexual activity. Sexual addicts often understand that what they are doing is wrong, and they do not understand why they feel so powerless to stop something so contrary to their moral beliefs.

Sexual addiction generally begins with a serious addiction to masturbation and possibly pornography. Some sexual addicts never move beyond this stage of addiction. Others progress to other forms of compulsive behavior. That addiction can take many different forms. Many addicts become sexually promiscuous. Some solicit prostitutes. Some expose themselves in public or peek through windows. In severe cases, the addict may commit rape or incest. Without professional help, the addiction most likely will not get better. It will often get worse.

Sexual addiction can be caused by many factors, from broken or dysfunctional families to early and/or frequent exposure to pornography. Sexual addicts are often attractive and very charming. They often "don't seem the type" to be involved in something as sleazy as porn shops or prostitution. They usually lead two lives, one as a respectable, maybe even a religious person, the other in the world of their addiction. In an effort to hide this double life, they are often dishonest and manipulative. They tend to blame others for their problems. They are often prone to anger. They frequently lose friends. And they are always very lonely people. Deep down they're not looking for sex, they're looking for intimacy.

Steven Arteburn writes:

> They wanted to be loved and accepted. Seeking relief from the pain of rejection, they betrayed their values, their morals, their very selves. Having been rejected by others, they came to reject themselves over the very behaviors they could not stop. Seeking acceptance, they ended up isolated from everyone.[1]

Sexual addicts can be helped through therapy—combined, of course, with prayer. Unfortunately, most addicts don't get help until they reach rock bottom—usually in the form of a divorce or arrest. But once they get that help, they can learn positive ways to achieve love and real intimacy and to let go of compulsive sexual behavior.

If you suspect someone you know of having a problem with compulsive sexual behavior, you cannot "fix" or "change" him—only a professional can do that. But you can confront him with your suspicions. Even if he reacts

---

[1] Arteburn, *Addicted to Love* (Ann Arbor, Mich.: Servant Publications, 1991), p. 115.

angrily, which he probably will, you have helped him to
see the problem. Help him understand it.

"What is the difference between sexual addiction and relationship addiction?"

Relationship addiction and sexual addiction often look very
much the same to an outsider. People with both kinds of
addiction are often sexually promiscuous. But while a sexual addict primarily seeks sexual release, a relationship addict hops from bed to bed in a futile attempt to find a relationship that will ease the pain in his life. The compulsion
appears similar to that of the sex addict, but it is actually
quite different.

Relationship addicts are not driven by sex per se. Often
they do not even particularly enjoy sex. Sex for them is
strictly a means to an end. If they believed they could have
that end—a loving relationship—without sex, they would
gladly forego sexual activity. But they do not believe they
can find love any other way.

The intended outcome for the sexual addict is only sexual release. Once that happens, the addict doesn't care if he
ever sees the sexual partner again. For a relationship addict,
however, the goal is to have an ongoing relationship with
the sexual partner—a relationship rarely if ever achieved.

As a rule, males with these types of problems tend to
be sexual addicts, while women tend to be relationship
addicts. Certainly there can be male relationship addicts
as well as female sex addicts. But these are the *tendencies*
for each gender. The important message is that there are
a lot of broken people out there, people who are trying

desperately to fulfill their needs in ways that don't work. These people need our love, our support and our prayers.

Like the sex addict, a relationship addict needs help. A competent Christian therapist can help him to understand the motivation behind this behavior and to find more positive ways of finding and expressing real love.

"If someone is a sexual or relationship addict, isn't prayer enough to cure them? Why does the person need a therapist?"

We should pray for healing for anyone suffering from any kind of addiction, as they should pray for themselves. Those prayers can be very powerful. But when someone has a stomach pain, he should supplement his prayer with a trip to the doctor's office. God may cure the problem through miraculous direct intervention, but it is far more likely that He will work through the skills and gifts of a doctor. The same applies to someone suffering from addiction. God brings about all healing. The sexual or relationship addict should certainly pray, but he should also consult a trained, *Christian* therapist who can act as God's instrument of healing.

Too Late?

"No one ever told me how special my virginity was and what a beautiful thing chastity is. Now it's too late. I just wish I could've heard you speak before, when I was younger and still very impressionable."

It is not too late. It is never too late. Chastity is about the present and future. Do not be imprisoned by your past. Repent, get on the bandwagon, and get on with your chaste future!

"I'm so mad now that I've been careless with my sexuality. I used to express my sexuality for guys because I wanted to show my love for them. Now I hardly even know them. This will be one of the hardest things in my life to do, but it will be one of the most fulfilling. Thank you."

No, thank *you*. Thanks to all of you who have heard the message of chastity, from me or someone else, and have decided to change your lives as a result of it. I respect, admire and love all of you more than you could ever know.

8

Walking the Walk

How Far Is Too Far?

"Exactly how far is too far? I've been wondering. Nobody really says. There are lots of steps between kissing and sex."

I particularly love this question and the questions that follow. There are many voices these days encouraging single people to abstain from sex. Unfortunately, very few will go the next step and help us with the nitty-gritty details of what chastity involves.

Many of these questions are questions I myself have asked. Straight answers are sometimes hard to find. I understand, however, the importance of answering these questions well. Remember, I am single, too. I strive to live chastity in my dating life. I am not asking you to follow any rules that I am not following myself. But it is important for all of us to understand *exactly* what chastity entails.

How far *can* you go and still be chaste? Does chastity mean you have to draw a line down the center of the room and keep your date on the opposite side? Or does it mean

186

that "anything goes" as long as there is no actual intercourse?

Neither. Chastity is simply about understanding the difference between affection and passion. Affection is good. We experience life through our bodies, so it is only fitting that we have bodily expressions for affection. Hugs, handholding and kisses can all be ways of expressing loving affection.

We get into trouble, however, when affection becomes passion. You all know what passion is—creating a desire for sexual intercourse or "turning someone on". Is that loving someone? Is that looking out for what is best for that person?

No. It is more like saying, "I love you so much, I am going to make you want something I am not going to give you." That is not loving. It is making it more difficult for that person to resist sexual temptation. It is leading him to frustration. This will not help your relationship.

There is nothing wrong with being sexually attracted to each other. That is good. But it is also a challenge—to keep your affection under control and to stop it before it becomes a temptation. When your affection starts leading to a desire to do more, then it is time to cool off—to go biking, or go out for ice cream, or *something* positive (and public).

What exact behaviors are on or off limits? We will be discussing those throughout the next several questions.

"Is petting a sin?"

For those of you who don't know what the word "petting" refers to in this context, it means touching, messing with or stimulating the private parts of someone else's body.[1] Those parts were made for sex, and messing with them is a part of sex. Messing with them outside of marriage is a sin in the same way sex outside of marriage is a sin.

I learned this pretty early on in my dating life. But I didn't learn why this kind of behavior is wrong. After all, you can't get pregnant that way. So what is so bad about it?

First of all, this is not a loving thing to do. Most of the risks we have discussed are present at that level. You are at risk of sexually transmitted disease. A certain level of bonding is definitely occurring. There is even a certain risk of pregnancy if you come into close enough contact. Putting yourself and someone else at that kind of risk is not loving.

Second, as we discussed in the last question, you are creating a desire in someone—a desire you don't intend to fulfill. These parts of the body were *designed* to create desire for sex. If a couple goes ahead and completes the act of intercourse, that pre-intercourse activity is no longer defined as "petting" but as "foreplay"—what they did to get in the mood for sex.

Is it smart to do this when you are not planning to keep going? Molly Kelly says that this would be like going out to the car, starting it, racing the engine for a while, then

---

[1] The parts that would've been covered by a bathing suit manufactured before 1964.

turning it off and going back inside. It makes very little sense.

Third, you are making it very difficult to stop. You were not made to stop after this kind of activity. It tends to "shut your brain down". I meet very upset people on an extremely regular basis; people who had no intention of going all the way but who got started in this kind of "affection" and didn't want to stop. (*Note:* This does not, repeat, *does not* mean that if you make a mistake and go this far, you have an excuse to go all the way. If you are not married, you need to muster all of your strength and quit, period. We now return to our regularly scheduled question.)

Fourth and most important, sex is the language of marriage. At what point does it begin to speak that language? When intercourse occurs? Or before?

To answer that question, you have to ask yourself another. If you were married and you found your spouse in bed naked with the next-door neighbor, would you be upset? Odds are, you would. "Oh, honey", your spouse would say. "It's not the way it looks. We're not going to go all the way." Would that make you feel better? I doubt it. Why? Because you would still feel that your marital sexual language had been violated.

There's another question to ask yourself. Think about your future spouse *now*, still single and out there dating. What don't you want him to do? Do you like the thought of your future wife getting hot and heavy in the back seat with some guy, or of that guy bragging about her in the locker room? Do you like the thought of your future husband in that kind of situation?

Look at your own date. This is somebody's future wife or husband. And your future spouse is probably going on similar dates. "Respect" means treating your dates the way you want your future spouse to be treated right now. Because if you are involved in sexual activity, even short of intercourse, you are violating your future marriage. You are cheating on your future spouse. You are cheapening the value of the future language of sex in your marriage.

I once talked to a woman who, while she had never "gone all the way" before her marriage, had gone fairly "far" in her dating affection. Her husband told her that she is the only woman he has ever kissed. She said to me, "I wish more than anything in the world I could say the same to him."

She realizes something that you will only fully realize after you are married. Sex speaks the language of marriage. And the arousal behavior leading up to sex speaks the same language. It is a language that, if you marry, you will share exclusively with your spouse. You won't like the thought of your spouse speaking it with someone else or remembering speaking it with someone else.

Sex is the language of marriage. Whatever you have done in the past, I challenge you today to make a decision to respect that language. Sex is a gift—a gift of yourself to your spouse. Don't "parcel it out" piece by piece to your dates over the years.

From now on, save it *all*—to give when the giving is right.

"Is oral sex considered actual sex and breaking chastity?"

Oral sex is a very serious sin against chastity, for the reasons described above.

Some people "rationalize" oral sex, thinking, "Well, it's not *really* having sex. I can do this and still be a virgin when I get married." Wrong attitude. It is intimate sexual behavior. It carries significant physical, emotional and spiritual risk. It is extremely dangerous in terms of exposure to sexually transmitted diseases; it can cause an emotional bond to form; and, like all serious sin, it cuts you off from God and can put your soul in serious jeopardy.

Oral sex is a very serious abuse of the language of sexuality. Don't do it.

"Is kissing on a date okay?"

"When should and shouldn't you kiss a girl?"

I once spoke to two different people about this subject in the same week. One was a young woman who said, "Oh, I'll kiss just about anyone if he's good looking." The other was a mother who told me about a young man at her daughter's school. He made it known that he didn't kiss the women he dates, because he thought kissing was something very special, and he wanted to wait for someone special to share it with.

Who would you rather be kissed by? Someone who will kiss "anyone" or someone who believes that kissing is something special?

191

A kiss can be a good thing. It is a way to express the way you feel about someone—it speaks a "language" of affection. So if you kiss someone, it should be a genuine expression of affection. You should not do it because you are bored, or because you are lonely and want to feel affection even if it is from someone you don't care about, or because you want to arouse that person or yourself sexually. That would be using this language in a lie.

If you feel honest affection for someone, but you are also feeling tempted to go farther than you should with this person, this would probably not be a good time to kiss him. Find another way to show your affection.

"If a guy takes me on a date, do I have to kiss him?"

You never, ever *have* to kiss anyone. There is absolutely no reason to kiss someone you barely know, or someone you do know but don't want to kiss. I don't care if he bought you a Coke or dinner or box seats at the Super Bowl—*you are never obligated to kiss anyone*. At the end of the date, you can just smile, say, "Thank you so much. It was a great evening. Good night" and go inside.

"Is making out okay?"

"Making out" is a broad phrase, which seems to cover everything from light kissing to heavy petting.

I know that when I was in high school, many of us held the attitude that if there was no actual "petting" going on, then everything else was fine. Couples could get as aroused as they wanted, as long as they didn't touch certain body parts.

Now how much sense does that make?

As I said before, *sincere* affection is good. It is expressing the way you feel about another person. But when you are kissing and hugging someone to whom you are sexually attracted, you need to be more than a little careful. Remember, the goal is to express *affection*, not to arouse sexually.

Common sense is the rule. If, in the course of your affection, you or your date are starting to want to do something you should not do, it is time to stop. You need to think about your limits, and what situations could be dangerous, *before* you get into those situations. People don't generally win any logic awards when they are already turned on. The brain is usually the first thing to go. Know your limits, and make them clear to your date.

The best advice, of course, is to spend your dating time doing *positive* things. Does "making out" help your relationship? Not really. You are not talking. You are not getting to know each other any better. Meanwhile, however, you are fueling a desire that you can't rightly satisfy. You are much better off spending your time getting to know each other and having a good time, instead of just "making out".

"Is French kissing okay?"

I spent *years* trying to get a straight answer to this question. Some priests said it was a sin. Some priests said it was an occasion of sin. Some said it was no big deal.

I finally got an answer from, of all places, a bridal shower. (Amazing, what a person can learn at those things.) We were talking about these kinds of dating-related issues, as single women sometimes do, and the bride said, "Well, we had to quit French kissing because I realized that was where I 'turn the corner' and start to think about wanting to go farther."

Here I was, worrying about whether it was a big sin, a little sin or no sin, and I forgot to think about, "Is this a good idea?" The idea of unmarried affection is to show just that—affection. But what effect does French kissing have? Does it help or hinder your efforts to be affectionate while maintaining a life of chastity? I think that it can tend to have a fairly arousing effect. This kind of activity is probably not going to help you to live chastity.

I strongly recommend that couples who want to live premarital chastity avoid French kissing. If you do this, you will probably be able to express sincere affection more easily without being as strongly tempted to go farther.

"What about . . . all of the other stuff?"

I realize that there are probably other sexual behaviors I have failed to mention specifically in this chapter, either because I am unaware of them or because some creative person just dreamed them up, or whatever. Just use your common sense. If the purpose of a particular activity is sexual arousal, and/or if it involves the private parts or functions of another person's body, then it is using another person, it is unchaste and you should not do it. Simple enough?

"How far *exactly* can we go?"

I have given you a lot of guidelines here, but some of you want more.

You want *exact* guidelines.

I am going to help you to answer your own question—in the form of a story.

Okay, you are a guy, and you have met the most wonderful woman in the world. She is beautiful, she is smart, she is funny, she is your best friend and your soul mate, and you can't believe how lucky you are to have her. You get married. She gets pregnant.

In the delivery room, you are the first one to see and to hold your little baby girl. She has your eyes and your wife's chin. She is perfect. You look at this little bundle, and you marvel at how something so beautiful could come from your love. You can't believe how much you love her.

You bring her home, and your wife dresses her in frilly dresses and tapes bows to her head because she doesn't have enough hair. She learns to walk the way toddlers do, leaning forward and catching themselves over and over again with their feet until they finally can't keep up and they fall. She picks flowers in the backyard and brings them to Daddy. When she learns to talk she says, "Da-da." When she cries, rocking with Daddy makes her feel better.

Now she goes to first grade. You walk her to school on the first day, and she cries because she is scared and doesn't want you to leave. But she comes home happy at the end of the day because she made an "I (backward L) Love You, Daddy" card.

Now she is in fourth grade. She has a piano recital, and

you leave work early to be there. She sees you from the piano bench and smiles. She plays the little song she wrote herself and dedicates it to Daddy.

Now she is in ninth grade, and she has a date. With a senior—who drives a van.

You tell me. How far is too far? How far do you want Mr. Senior-with-a-Van to go with your little girl? Do you want him to do everything he can possibly get away with short of intercourse? I doubt it.

Here is the bottom line, for both men and women. You are living chastity when you treat your dates the way you want Mr. Senior to treat your little girl. Period. That is real love. That is looking out for the best for the other person.

Fantasy, Pornography and Masturbation

**"Is it wrong to fantasize about having sex?
I mean, all of the time."**

All of the time, huh? Hmmm.

It is true that chastity is not just about what we do or don't do. Chastity starts inside of us, in our brains. It starts with how we think. We can be impure in our thoughts just as we can be impure in our actions.

I remember first hearing the Christian injunction against "impure thoughts". I thought it was pretty weird. I thought that premarital sex was wrong because I could get pregnant or hurt somehow. I was fairly certain that I could not get pregnant just thinking about sex. It is difficult to use someone or to lead someone on if no one else is actually involved. But as usual, I hung on to the teaching and figured that the Church was right. Sure enough, now I can see why.

First of all, we all have to define what we mean by "thinking about sex". We don't mean thinking about why God created sex, what a precious gift sex is, or how you are saving sex for marriage. Those are all good things to think about. An "impure thought", on the other hand, means actually, explicitly, imagining doing sexual things and getting sexual pleasure out of those thoughts.

Does this mean that you commit a sin every time a sexual image pops into your head? Of course not. You are a human being. Sexual thoughts will often pop into your mind uninvited—that is a part of being human. In addition, we live in a society that is full of sexually stimulating images. You would have to hide in your basement to avoid sexual images completely. You are made to respond to sexual stimuli, and often the stimulus is not willed and the response is automatic. You can't control what pops into your brain.

What we are talking about here—what you can control —is what you do when something "pops into your brain". Martin Luther once said, "You can't keep birds from flying around your head, but you can stop them from making a nest in your hair." When a sexual feeling or image pops into your mind, do you say, "Okay, so I am a sexual being" and go on about your day? Or do you say, "Wow, that feels good" and think about it for the next half hour?

Once you make a conscious decision to think about sexual acts and enjoy the resulting arousal, you are in the realm of impure thoughts.

What is wrong with that? Does it hurt anyone? Yes. First of all, it hurts you. This kind of daydreaming makes you a less chaste person with a less chaste attitude. Doing this will hurt your efforts at chastity. How? Let's say that you were on a diet, but you spent a lot of time thinking about sundaes and doughnuts and how good they taste. What would you do the next time there was a sundae in front of you? You would want to eat it. It would be a lot more difficult to resist. The same thing goes for sex. If you have spent all your time thinking about how much you want to do it, you are going to have a very difficult time resisting when temptation rolls around.

Second, when you are fantasizing, you are not using sex the way it was intended to be used. What is sex? Communication—a communication of marital love. But with whom are you communicating? No one. What could you possibly be communicating? You are all alone. Sex then becomes directed inward, a selfish drive to be satisfied by an imaginary person who "exists" only to please you. You don't have to and, in fact, *can't* care about this person. You are contributing to an unchaste, "using" mentality toward sex.

There is a third way that sexual "imaginings" can hurt us. They can do profound damage to our real relationships, both present and future. No matter how hard you try, you can't "imagine" what marital sexual expression would be like. It would be like trying to imagine a conversation in your mind. All the words are yours. Likewise, when we imagine sexual activity, our fantasy is not realistic. The other person is not present. There is no interaction. The focus is only on ourselves and our pleasure. Trying to do this can easily lead to selfishness and to unrealistic expectations about marital sexuality.

In the imagination, there is no such thing as gravity, drafty rooms, headaches or fights. In the imagination, every woman's face is on Cindy Crawford's body.

Too much time with a Victoria's Secret catalogue and an active imagination can, on the physical level, lead to a very disappointing honeymoon. Another person is present, whose wishes and needs may clash with your fantasized reality. And women are made to store fat in certain places —fat that sometimes doesn't disappear despite years of step aerobics and Ultra Slim-Fast.

What is worse than disappointment, however, is that all of that fantasizing can fixate you on the physical and blind you to the spiritual and emotional realities that God is working in your marriage. Here is another individual, another image of God, who has bound his life to yours forever out of love for you. God is present, sanctifying your love and working through it to make your love fruitful. Sexual union is an expression of your commitment to each other, to God and to whatever children you may bring into the world. Sex is not about performance or physical beauty. It is about loving openness to God and each other.

Too much daydreaming can fixate you on the physical and blind you to the beauty of the spiritual.

I heard not long ago about a man who, six weeks after his wife bore their child, refused to resume their sexual relationship because she had not yet lost her last five "pregnancy pounds". This is a guy who has apparently spent entirely too much time daydreaming. He has been blinded to the awesome, sacred reality of sexuality in God's plan, and he is missing out.

What should we do about all of this now, as single people? First of all, we recognize that sexual attraction exists, often between people who are not married. That is good —it is how we were made. But we can experience the true, full meaning of sexual union only by saving it for the context for which it was made—marriage. It is normal to be curious and to wonder what it would be like. But to try to imagine marital sex would be, as Walter Trobisch once said, like trying to imagine what it is like to be dead by sleeping very soundly.[2] It can't be done. And you can't seek its pleasures without stealing from the future.

Sometimes I know it is easy to start daydreaming about sex when you are bored or having problems or wanting to escape a situation. But fantasizing won't help. The best way to gain maturity is to stay in reality, deal with whatever situations you may face, and save sex for the future when it can mean what it is supposed to mean.

"Is masturbation a sin?"

Masturbation is wrong for the same reasons listed in the last question. In fact, you should probably reread that entire answer and use it to answer this question.

Sex is meant to be a loving communication between two people. Masturbation short-circuits that process. That is why it is often a very lonely activity. Masturbation doesn't

---

[2] Walter Trobisch, *I Loved a Girl* (San Francisco: HarperCollins, 1989), p. 7.

help you to become a more chaste, more loving person. It conditions you to associate sex with pleasure for yourself only.

Masturbation, when done with full knowledge and consent of the will, is a sin. I realize that masturbation can be a fairly easy habit to fall into, particularly for adolescent boys. The habit, like other sexual habits, can be fueled by other underlying issues—loneliness, lack of real love, and so forth. The force of that habit and those underlying issues that fuel it can decrease an individual's moral responsibility for the sin. The best thing to do in this situation is to pray, to strive to identify and address any underlying causes, and to work diligently to break the habit. This is not something you will be able to do alone. You absolutely *need* to find a good confessor—a priest whom you trust completely, who understands the problem, and who wants to help you. As I have said before, he doesn't need to know your name, but if you are not going face to face, he should have some way of identifying you as the same person each time. It is easiest to tell him at least your first name. Remember, you certainly won't shock him. This is an *extremely* common issue for confessors.

In addition to your confessor, there may be someone else you trust who would be willing to help you talk through some of these issues. If this is the case, by all means go ahead. There is also an excellent book on the subject called *My Beautiful Feeling*, by Walter and Ingrid Trobisch.

I receive letters periodically from people who are actually *addicted* to masturbation. This, as you may recall, is the first stage of sexual addiction. These people tell me that their addiction has damaged and in some cases ended their marriages. They are very unhappy and wish they had dealt with the problem while it was still manageable. If you believe that you may have reached this level of compulsion, tell your confessor, or call one of the numbers given in Appendix 2 below.

"Is it a sin to look at pornography?"

"Do you think pornography is wrong in helping aroused men to calm their hormones?"

You show me a man whose hormones are *calmed* by pornography, and I will show you a highly unusual man.

Pornography is not designed to calm hormones—it is designed to arouse them. Yes, that is a sin. This is again closely connected to the last two questions.

Sex is meant to be a language of communication of love between a man and a woman who know each other and give themselves to each other for life. Pornography turns that gift upside down. It features provocative pictures of unrealistically perfect bodies, and it is designed only to arouse sexually.

Pornography is extremely dangerous to chastity on a multitude of levels. It is about use—about becoming sexually aroused by someone with whom you have no relationship, someone you don't even know. The women and men pictured are not seen as the individuals they are, created in the image and likeness of God, but as mere objects of your own personal satisfaction. That is use, and it is wrong.

Pornography teaches its audiences to use, not to love. It

is impossible to learn both lessons simultaneously. Someone who is conditioned to being stimulated by pornography will not be able suddenly to engage in selfless, self-giving marital lovemaking. It just doesn't work that way.

Pornography also creates highly unrealistic expectations about sex. No one looks like the people in those pictures —not even the people in those pictures. The photos are airbrushed. Your spouse, on the other hand, will not be airbrushed. It's not fair to create such an unrealistic expectation in your mind. That expectation will be there, whether you want it to be or not.

Sexual images are very strong. They burn into the mind in a way that very few other images do. Once they are in there, they never go away. They come back when you don't need them—when you are trying to be chaste, for instance.

Pornography is dangerous. Since there is no self-giving love, there is none of the *real* satisfaction that marital sex is supposed to give. Eventually pornography fails to stimulate at all. Then some users of pornography get bored and move on to "harder stuff" to get the same thrill. Hard-core pornography is about cruelty and violence. It is about sex crimes. This kind of pornography breaks down the reader's aversion to acts of sexual violence. Virtually all convicted "sex offenders" are avid consumers of pornography.

Don't put those images in your brain. If you have pornographic materials in your possession, burn them now, and start praying and working to regain the virtue of chastity. If you are dating someone who is in any way involved in pornography, do not stick around. For him (or her) to enjoy that stuff, even the "mild" stuff like *Playboy*, is abusive to you, and it will keep this person from ever loving you the way you should be loved. Get out.

I remember years ago learning that a certain man I knew had a subscription to *Playboy*. I thought, "Well, I guess all guys are like that." Guess what? They aren't. Hold out for one who isn't.

"How about trashy romance novels? Do they lower your chastity?"

Good question! Yes, they can, in a couple of ways. First, these books function in much the same way pornography does—stimulating the reader sexually outside of the context of a loving, marital sexual relationship. They may not be *as* damaging, because they don't directly flash physical images into the brain, but they are dangerous nonetheless.

Romance novels, like pornography, create unrealistic expectations. These expectations may not be of the physical type, but they are real nonetheless. They depict an unrealistic world of perfect men (all of whom are named "Thor" and look like Fabio), beautiful women and unending romance. Guess what? The real world isn't like that.

Believe it or not, there are actually people who undergo treatment for addiction to romance novels. They live for this kind of "literature" (I use the term loosely), and they can't function in the world of real relationships any more because that world is not "perfect" like their books.

The moral to this and the preceding questions is simple: Live your life in reality. Don't try to escape into fantasy, or masturbation, or pornography, or trashy novels. None of that stuff will help you in the end. It can only hurt your ability to live chastity and to find real, honest love.

Dressing for Chastity

"What clothes do you consider too revealing to wear because they might tempt a guy?"

Another good question!

A lot of women do not understand the issue of modesty. They say, "I will wear whatever I want, and if a guy has a problem with it, that's his problem."

The problem, and it is a problem a lot of women are not aware of, is that men and women are "wired" very differently. Men tend to be very visually oriented. They are more affected by what they *see*. This is particularly true in the realm of sexuality. The sight of the female body can be very sexually arousing to them.

Women are a little bit different. Sure, women appreciate a well-built male form. But they are not affected visually in the same intense way that men are. Women are stimulated primarily through touch and through what we hear. Words of love and tenderness in the context of an intimate relationship are much more stimulating to women than what they see.

So when women say "If he has a problem with the way I'm dressed, that's his problem", they say that because they don't understand why the way they dress would be such a problem to a man. They have personally never experienced this kind of problem.

But for guys it *is* a problem. This is not to say that they are perverts or sex maniacs. It just means that men are wired that way. They didn't ask to be like this. Many of them would probably prefer *not* to be so visually oriented. But they can't help it. They are stimulated by what they see.

To put it simply, it is not *nice* to do this to a guy. It is difficult enough to live chastity. Men don't need women to be dressing in a way that makes chastity even more difficult for them. That is not helping them, and it is not loving them.

Many "good" guys, guys who strive to live chastity, have told me that when a woman is dressed immodestly, her clothes (or the lack thereof) get in the way of being able to get to know her as a person. A woman is not a collection of "parts". She is a whole individual, a soul and a personality and unique image and likeness of God, all wrapped up in a body. But if she is dressed in such a way that emphasizes her sexual "parts", that is very distracting to a man, whether he wants it to be or not. Those parts just keep screaming out for attention and distract him from getting to know *her*.

So, women, which would you prefer? A man looking at you saying, "She seems like a very nice person. I would like to get to know her better", or someone looking at you and immediately thinking about sex. I know which I would prefer.

Dressing modestly does not, repeat, *does not* mean dressing unattractively. It is good to dress attractively. God gave us our bodies—they have dignity. We want to reflect that in the way we present ourselves to the world. But dressing modestly means dressing to show off your *whole self*, not just dressing to call attention to the sexual parts of your body. Let your inner self shine through by the way you dress, not become obscured by it.

What clothes are too revealing? That is a difficult question to answer across the board. Certainly anything that exposes or calls undue attention to the private parts of the body is immodest. Other clothes can also be immodest. The best way to tell is to choose a man, someone whom you trust, with whom you are not romantically involved and who understands and lives chastity (brothers can be helpful here, if they are chaste), and to ask *him* if your clothes are modest or if they are distracting.

If he gives an outfit the "thumbs down", take it back. It is not worth keeping.

Chastity Guidelines

"What would be appropriate or inappropriate behavior in leading a chaste life?"

We have just listed several ways to help yourself live chastity. Avoid petting. Avoid arousing each other. Avoid pornography, fantasy and masturbation. Dress modestly.

I have, however, a few more suggestions:

1. *Know your limits:* You need to decide *in advance* what is acceptable and unacceptable behavior. That does not mean, "Well, heavy petting is okay, but not intercourse." It means

knowing what situations will tempt you to sexual behavior and avoiding them. If, for example, being in a dark room alone used to lead to sexual intercourse and being there makes you want to do it again, you should probably avoid dark rooms.

Likewise, you need to know and *believe* that unchaste behavior is bad. Then you need to act accordingly. When someone "puts a move on you", you need to intercept it. Immediately. It is easy, when you are in that situation, to think, "He's just doing this because he loves me." Maybe he loves you, but what he is doing is not loving behavior. It is exploitative. You need to make a decision: "Touch me there, and I go home." And then follow through. If he or she doesn't listen the next time, you should say "Touch me there again, and I go home for good." The same goes for someone who is pressuring you or trying to seduce you. There is no reason to hang around.

2. *Be selective about dating:* Dating is probably the single most overrated activity in the history of the universe. On TV, single people date constantly, and we feel like something is wrong with us if we don't date that often, too.

Puhleeease!! If there is no one around you want to date, what is the point? If a person isn't going to respect your sexuality and your limits, what is the point? You don't need to date just for the sake of dating. In the end, the most important relationships in your life are going to be your friendships, both male and female. And you will have a lot more fun with friends than you will have dating someone you don't like or who doesn't respect you. Save dates for special people whom you respect and who respect you.

3. *Be sure there is plenty of real love in your life:* Maintaining strong, loving relationships with your family and friends is without a doubt one of the best ways to maintain chastity. As we have seen, much of today's sexual activity is fueled by a hunger for love. If your "tank" is full, you won't be as tempted to look for counterfeit love in sexual relationships.

4. *Learn about chastity:* I know that, after reading this book, you feel that you have learned all there is to know about the subject. But guess what? There is more. Keep reading. Read the books listed in the Bibliography. They are my personal favorites, and I am sure they will help you.

The more you understand, the stronger you will be.

5. *Stay close to God:* Chastity is difficult in this day and age. If you try to live chastity without God, I absolutely guarantee that you will fail. His grace provides the fuel you need to resist the temptations that will come your way on a daily basis.

Pray daily for chastity. Pray for an understanding of it. Pray for the strength to live it.

Occasions of Sin

"What is an 'occasion of sin'?"

An "occasion of sin" is an action or a situation that is not necessarily a sin in itself but that might tempt you to sin. For instance, it is not a sin to go into a dark room. (If it were, photographers would have a real problem.) But if you are with someone to whom you are sexually attracted, and when you go into a dark room with that person you get very tempted to do sexual things, then it would be an occasion of sin for you to go into that dark room.

If there is a situation you *know* is an occasion of sin for you, you know you have sinned in that situation in the past, and you know that if you go into that situation again, you will probably be tempted and sin again, then it can be a sin just to go into that situation in the first place. It is just not smart. You are flirting with danger.

Sex and Alcohol

"How are alcohol and sex connected?"

In the land of threats to chastity, alcohol is king. Alcohol shuts down your brain, or at least the part of your brain that makes good, loving decisions. It leaves only the drives, which know only pizza love—"want what I want when I want it". What our drives often want is sex, especially when we are with people to whom we are attracted.

As I said in the last chapter, I can't begin to tell you the number of young men and women I have spoken with and cried with. They understood and embraced chastity. They wanted to live it. They were saving sex for marriage. But they got drunk and made a mistake, and now they are miserable. Some are pregnant. Some have diseases. All are profoundly disappointed.

Don't think "I'm too strong for that." No one is. It doesn't work that way. Alcohol takes away that strength.

And you don't have to be "drunk" to lose control. Even a drink or two can lower your resistance.

Take my advice—don't drink and date. It is way too dangerous.

Sleeping Together

"What about just sleeping together (no sex)?"

Bad idea.

Think about "sleeping". You are lying down together. You are in extremely close physical proximity for a long period of time. You are in a bed, which for obvious reasons is associated with sex in many people's minds. You are generally wearing loose clothing.

This in itself can be a fairly arousing situation. Combine that situation with the fact that you are drifting in and out of consciousness, and you are not always completely in control of your actions, and you have a recipe for serious trouble.

Do you honestly believe that you can be in a situation like this, with someone to whom you are sexually attracted, for any period of time without getting into some kind of trouble? I highly doubt it. Maybe the first night it will be okay. Maybe it won't. But eventually, after not very many nights, you are going to have a problem. I can almost guarantee it. This is an "occasion of sin" if I have ever seen one.

I *strongly* urge you to avoid "sleeping together" until you are married. Waking up in the morning with your spouse is special. Don't make your husband or wife just another person who has been in your bed.

Dealing with Desire

"Is it wrong for a guy to have a physical attraction toward a woman?"

No, no, no. As I have said before, physical attraction is good. It is the way you were made. Sometimes physical attraction is part of a larger overall attraction to a person. Sometimes it is isolated, as in the case of a beautiful actress or a photo of an attractive person. Either way, sexual attraction is not something you can consciously choose. Sometimes, attraction just happens.

But you can control what you do about it. Don't let it overwhelm your thinking or your judgment. Don't initiate physical activity just to feed the physical attraction. Get to know the *person*, and then see what happens to the attraction.

"Is it wrong to want to have sex before marriage?"

Define "want". If you mean "to have a physical urge to have sex" or "to want to give myself totally to someone I am in love with", then it is perfectly normal. Those desires were put there by God as opportunities for us to learn to become loving persons. When you say, "I *really* want to make love to you, but because it is not what's best for you, I won't", you are being a loving person, and you are growing in chastity. That is good.

If by "want" you mean "deciding that we should have sex even though we're not married and pressuring my boyfriend or girlfriend to do it", then yes, it is wrong. You can't decide what your body will or will not want, but you can decide how you will respond. And deciding to put someone else at risk to satisfy that urge is wrong.

"If someone really wants to have sex, what do they do for quenching the urge?"

"What should we do in times of *high* temptation?"

"How do I control lust? The problem is, I really don't want to. What do I do?"

I like these questions. They are all very *real*.

The urge for sex can be very, very strong sometimes—often when you least expect it. It wouldn't be very nice of me to ask you to live chastity and then not to help you deal with temptation.

Sexual energy is just that—energy. Sometimes we have very little of it, and other times we have a *lot* of it. The beauty of *human* sexuality, however, is that we are the only creatures made by God who can "sublimate" that energy. In other words, we can take that energy and use it in other, nonsexual activities, like playing sports, cleaning or tackling homework. This is why every high school since the beginning of time has had an athletics program. These programs were not designed because someone invented the trophy case and wanted to fill it. They exist to give teenagers a way to work off all the sexual energy they are experiencing.

If you are alone and you are sexually tempted, there are three things you need to do. First is to say, "Okay, I am a sexual human being and I am being tempted. I am normal." Then say a quick prayer for chastity. Then go do something else. Call a friend. Go out on your bike. Bake cookies. Occupy your mind and use that energy doing something positive.

If you are with someone else, the steps are slightly different. First, don't bother talking to yourself. Go straight to the prayer for chastity. Then, if you are engaging in affectionate behavior, *stop* immediately. It is not helping you. Either go immediately into a public place or end the date altogether. Sometimes it is better to spend a few minutes in a public place together before going home just so the other person is not left suddenly alone and bewildered. But whatever you do, do not go back into a private situation where you could get into trouble.

The key to all of this is energy, not repression. You are not trying to take all of this energy and stuff it back down. You are trying to release that energy in a nonsexual way. If you are involved in some intense, nonsexual, energy-expending activity, you will be much less likely to give in to temptation.

"Sometimes I get tempted just from seeing my girlfriend, and we're not even doing anything. Is that normal?"

That is perfectly normal. Sometimes, especially when you love someone, "high temptation" can occur as soon as you *see* each other, right there at the front door. I have known engaged couples who have spent their entire engagement time together at Denny's. That's okay. The important thing is, once again, "know thyself." If you are already feeling tempted, don't feed it. Do other things together, but don't get into situations where you are going to be even *more* tempted.

"If you are friends with a girl and you start to have sexual feelings for her, should you talk about it with her or just force it on her?"

I am not making this up. This is an actual question submitted to me during a question-and-answer period.

I hope by now the answer is obvious. You should never, *ever* force *anything* on *anyone*. This is assault. It is illegal, as well as immoral, sinful and highly unchaste.

Now, with that out of the way, let's get on with what you should do. First of all, what are these feelings exactly? Are these sexual feelings part of a larger attraction to her as a person and an interest in pursuing a romantic relationship with her and exploring the possibility of spending the rest of your lives together? If so, then you should talk to her and see if she shares those feelings. If she does, then perhaps you can begin to change your relationship from "friendship" to "dating". If she doesn't share your feelings, at least you know where she stands and you can get on with your life and date other people.

Or are these feelings just "sexual", a normal male attraction to a female body, but without any interest in her as a potential dating partner or future wife? If that is the case, then the best thing to do is nothing. You don't need to tell her, unless these feelings are becoming a problem for you. Otherwise, just continue to be her friend, but keep it very platonic. Don't get into sexually tempting situations with her, and don't fantasize about her. Just try to appreciate her as a person, and be the best friend to her that you possibly can.

"What if you can't say 'no'?"

This can be a real situation. Imagine liking someone a lot. Imagine wanting more than anything in the world to be this person's boyfriend or girlfriend. Then imagine being on a date with this person. If he or she were to pressure you for sex, could you say "no" and be firm about it, knowing that it may mean losing your only chance ever to have the kind of relationship you want with this person? Would you be strong enough to look this person straight in the eye and say "no" and watch him or her walk permanently out of your life? Think about it, and answer the question honestly.

If the answer is that you would not be strong enough to say "no" to this person, then you have learned one thing. You are not old enough, or mature enough, to be dating. There is nothing wrong with being young or immature. That is what youth is all about. But don't at the same time be complaining, "My parents won't let me date because they say I am not old enough."

It requires a *lot* of maturity and self-possession to be able to risk a relationship by saying "no" to someone. If you don't have that maturity and self-possession, then you are not mature enough to date. I don't care if you are thirty. You are not ready.

"What if you think you really love him, and you're all hot and bothered and you don't want to stop?"

There are a couple of problems with this scenario right away. First of all, you *think* you love him? Sex is an expression of, "I am so sure I love you that I have given myself to you permanently in the sacrament of marriage." It certainly doesn't say, "I *think* I love you."[3]

Second, you are already "hot and bothered". Why did you go and do that? Of course you don't want to stop *after* you have gotten hot and bothered. That is the whole point of stopping before you get to that point.

If, however, you get to the point where you *are* tempted to go farther, you should pray and then gather every ounce of energy you have and *stop. Immediately.* Go to a public place. Go home. Run and run fast. Do not hang around, because the longer you stay, the tougher it will be to resist.

---

[3] Only David Cassidy says that.

Saying "No"

"Is there any specific way to avoid sex but stay in a relationship if one person is pressuring the other for sex?"

That depends on the person doing the pressuring. If he or she is willing to stop pressuring and to live chastity out of respect for you, then you should have no problem.

If, on the other hand, the pressuring party doesn't accept "no" for an answer, you are not dealing with a person who respects you. *Don't* stick around with someone who is pressuring you sexually. This person does *not* love you and is *not* looking for what is best for you. Maybe he or she is just too immature to be able to love. But, regardless, there is no reason to stay with someone who doesn't love you—particularly if that person is pressuring you for sex. That pressure will become more and more difficult to resist. If you think it is difficult to leave now, I assure you that it will be a lot more difficult after you have given in to the pressure.

"After hearing this talk, I've realized that my girlfriend and I have to stop having sex. I want to tell her, but I'm afraid that I'll lose her. How can I explain this to her?"

Very, very lovingly. Explain that you have realized some things about sex that you didn't realize before. Tell her that it is clear to you that sex is putting her, you and your relationship at risk, and that you don't want to do that anymore. Tell her that it is *because* you care about her, and because the relationship is important to you, that you don't want to jeopardize anything. Tell her that this is very important to you. Be firm but loving.

I realize that it can be very, very scary to tell someone that your sexual activity has to stop. It is an accurate, but frightening, test. In doing this, you find out how a person *really* feels about you. You find out if it is you she loves or just sex.

If she listens, if she understands and if she accepts your wishes, then you will know that it is *you* she is interested in. If, on the other hand, she doesn't respect your wishes, if she threatens to leave unless you continue to have sex with her, then it is pretty clear where her priorities are. It hurts to find out, to be sure, but it is better to find out now than to wait until it is too late.

Of course, making her understand is just the first step. Next, and more challenging, is actually to live out that new commitment. For help in doing that, see the previous chapter.

"How do you tell a guy what you will and will not do sexually?"

If you are not married to him, "will not" covers everything he needs to know.

How do you tell him? First of all, I am sure you have told him a lot about what you won't do without even knowing it, before he even asked you out. The way you dress, the way you present yourself, the way you talk—all of these speak volumes about you. Men can read that language. If you are giving a clear, consistent message that you respect yourself, that you respect the gift of sexuality and that you don't consider sex a plaything, then don't be surprised if the guys who are looking for sex don't ask you out. Consider it a compliment.

Second, be picky about your dates. You don't have to go out with everyone who asks. If a guy has a reputation for being a "player" or for being sexually promiscuous, or if you know he has put pressure on other women, why on *earth* would you want to go out with him? It would be a waste of time at best and a dangerous situation at worst. Stick with men you know to be good guys.

Once you are on the date, you can send still more messages. Dress attractively but modestly. Don't tell dirty jokes, and don't respond if he does. You don't have to force the issue, but if the subject of sexuality comes up in conversation (in this day and age, it almost certainly will sometime in the first few dates), share your views.

Keep control of your affection. There is no reason to get too "affectionate" with someone you don't know very well anyway, so this shouldn't be a problem on the first few dates. By the time you feel you know him well enough to kiss him, he should know you well enough to know your views on chastity.

If he's *still* dense enough to try something, see the next question.

"How do you say 'no' without sounding stupid
or wrecking your relationship?"

"What's the best way to tell a guy 'no'?"

"Can you give some more neutral things
to say to a guy in the back seat other than,
'Excuse me, let's be chaste'?"

I listed three different versions of this question to illustrate
the point that I get a *lot* of questions like this. ("Excuse
me, let's be chaste" is my personal favorite.) It is clear to
me that a *lot* of single people struggle with this.

It can be difficult to say "no". Important, but difficult.
That is why it is important to try not to get to the point
where you will have to say "no" in the first place. You
can do that, as I said in the last question, by being careful
about whom you date, by giving consistent messages and
by being clear in your views.

First of all, you don't owe anybody anything except the
word "no", stated clearly and firmly. It is *your* body, after
all. Your date has no *rights* over it—I don't care how long
you have been together. Sometimes someone will try to
pressure you by arguing. I always felt like I had to write a
thirty-word essay: *Why My Virginity Is Important to Me, by
Mary Beth*. Dates sometimes think that if they can out-argue
you, they will "win". That is wrong. Don't get sucked into
this kind of argument.

If you want to explain more about the beauty and the
importance of chastity, that's fine. Go ahead. But do not,
repeat, *do not* try to explain it while you are in the "back

221

seat" (where you probably shouldn't have gone in the first place), or in any other remotely tempting situation. Go home and call him on the phone. *Then* explain it.

Date Rape

"What should you do in a situation of date rape (before it happens)?"

Date rape is a horrible, disgusting crime. Like any other form of rape, it can leave emotional scars that last a long, long time.

If you have taken the steps listed above, you are well on your way to avoiding date rape. Give consistent messages that you are not sexually available, and avoid dating men who you know have put pressure on other women.

Be very careful about whom you date. Meeting men on the street or in bars may seem exciting, but it is actually *very* dangerous. Never go out with a man whom neither you, nor anyone you know, knows anything about. If someone asks you out, always check with people you trust who know him well. If no such person exists, pass on the offer.

On the first few dates, stay in public places. Don't invite him into your home. If you live alone or with roommates, don't tell him where you live. Meet him at the restaurant, and bring your own car. If he ever makes you feel uncomfortable or frightened in any way, leave immediately. You don't have to stick around. If you need an excuse, say you don't feel well. (At that point, that is probably a true statement.) Then get out of there.

I know all of this may seem paranoid, but there are just enough lunatics out there to make a woman wary. Don't be too naïve or trusting right away. It could hurt you.

Getting Out

"I'm in a relationship that we've had sex in—I don't have any idea how to get out. Help!"

Any breakup is tough, but the breakup of a sexual relationship is infinitely more difficult. We discussed breaking up before, and we will discuss it again, but I will review some of the highlights again here.

First of all, make a firm decision and stick with it. If you are sure you want out, then trust that certainty. You will need confidence in your decision, because at some point in the future, when you are feeling weak and lonely, you will probably be tempted to go back to him for security. When that happens, remember the certainty you now have and don't go back.

Second, make a clean break. Don't say, "Maybe we should cool off for a while" or "let's see other people". You are certain that you want to end it, so do it quickly and honestly. It is not fair to him to drag it out.

Don't play the "let's be friends" game right away. I know you have probably heard a lot of people say that you can be friends with your ex's. I myself have several ex-boyfriends who are wonderful, treasured friends. But we were not good friends right away after we broke up. More importantly, we never had sex, and that makes a big difference.

I am extremely pessimistic about the possibility of being friends with someone with whom you have had sex, especially if he was your first.

For now, you need to be away from him—totally and completely. No phone calls, no letters, no nothing. If you need the security and intimacy he provided, then you need to find out exactly how badly you need it, and you need to find other ways to fulfill that need. Without doing that, you are *addicted* to him, and that is no good. Later, you may be able to be friends. But not now.

There is no easy way to do this. It will hurt sometimes. But as we said in the last chapter, there is good pain and there is bad pain. Staying in an unhealthy relationship is bad pain—it will never get any better. Leaving is good pain. It will help you to find out what "needs" were keeping you with him and free you to meet those needs without needing him.

So be brave and go!

College

"In college, there is so much more pressure to have sex. I don't think it's possible to find a guy who won't break up with you in college if you don't have sex with him. It seems as if all college relationships include sex."

There is a lot of pressure to have sex in college. You are on your own. You see yourself as an "adult" for the first time. You want to do what adults do, and they don't just have "boyfriends" or "girlfriends". Adults have "affairs", right? At least that's the way it is on TV.

To complicate all of this, you have roommates, most of whom have elaborate systems for keeping each other out of the room while they are having sex. Socks on the doorknob, "call Aunt Martha" notes on the door, or any one of a number of signals can be used to guarantee privacy. You have health centers that pass out contraceptives as if they were candy. Fraternities consistently host "women drink free" parties.[4]

All of this means that you must be very careful when you get into college. Don't let yourself be sucked into the mind-set you may see around you.

But all is not lost. Not *all* college relationships include sex. None of mine did, and I had several. Most of my friends also abstained from sex throughout their college relationships. As I speak at colleges all over the country, I constantly meet very wonderful, impressive college men who understand and live chastity. Several campuses are actually forming chastity support clubs. I have seen a few of these campus groups myself, and I have been extremely impressed.

It also helps to go to a college where the odds will be better. A *truly* Catholic or other Christian campus will undoubtedly have far more students who understand and embrace chastity. They won't *all* live it, of course, but the odds will be better.

---

[4] I used to think that these parties were evidence that chivalry was not dead. I was pretty naïve in my day.

I spent my first two years of college at a big state school —Colorado State University. There were men on that campus who respected sex—not *thousands* of them, but I met several, and they were all great guys. I was, however, very lonely in my faith there. My junior year I transferred to a smaller, Catholic program—the St. Ignatius Institute at the University of San Francisco. After I transferred, I was *much* happier—not just in terms of dating, but on every level. If you are choosing a college, you may want to look at some smaller, Catholic schools. It is much easier to learn, and to date, when you are surrounded by people who share your faith.

In short, don't give up. There are good guys on college campuses. And even if there weren't, that would be no reason to throw in the towel and stop living chastity. You are worth more than that.

Sexually Active Friends

"I have a friend who says she has decided to have sex with her boyfriend. How do I discourage her?"

Another question I hear a lot, and a difficult one.

First and foremost, pray for her. Pray that she will be open to the message of chastity. Pray that she will respect the gift and dignity of her sexuality. Pray that you will have the right words to tell her about it.

Then talk to her. Try to learn all you can about chastity first, but don't take too long if she is about to do something. (If you've read the book this far, you are off to a good start.)

Start by asking her a few questions. Why is she doing this? What does she hope to gain? As she answers, listen carefully.

Then try to explain chastity to her. Everyone is different, so you will need to decide which aspect of chastity would be most effective to emphasize to her. Does she believe in God? Tell her about the beauty of His creation. Would fear of AIDS or STD or pregnancy be enough to get her to think twice? Maybe she is looking for love, and you could help her to see that she won't find it this way.

While you are talking to her, be sure to remain loving and concerned. Remember that this is about her and about wanting what is best for her. Make sure she sees that.

Offer her this book or another book or video. If there is a chastity lecture in your area, invite her to go with you. Don't "pressure" her, but make it clear to her that you love her very much and that you are worried about her.

If she does it anyway, don't cut her off. You don't have to pretend to approve, and in fact you shouldn't. But remain a presence in her life. There may be pain down the road, and she is going to need a friend. Be there for her, and pray for her.

Holding out for Good Guys

"Do you receive a lot of grief from guys, etc., because you want to be chaste?"

"Now that you are an adult, do the men you get into relationships with think you are strange because you practice chastity?"

Like everyone else who lives chastity, I meet plenty of men who don't see things my way. Fortunately, I have a very good weeding system for dates. It goes like this:

Him: "What do you do for a living?"

Me: "I tell single people not to have sex until they're married."

Any man who is still standing there at the end of the sentence is the kind of man I want to date. He is probably going to respect me. Obviously, guys who are after sex are way too smart ever to ask me out. It would be a clear waste of their time.

So, as a result, I tend to date men who respect what I am doing. There are plenty of men like that in the world. I may not date quite as often as the average single television character does, but the quality is always high.

As the old saying goes, "If you expect only the best, very often you will find that you get it."

I am not going to "cave in" just to get a date. You shouldn't, either.

9

Men and Women

Emotions

"Why aren't guys as emotional as women?"

This is a fairly common assumption—that men are not "emotional", that their feelings are not as deep or as intense as women's feelings.

I happen to believe that this assumption is wrong.

In both my personal and professional life, I have had the immense privilege of coming to know many very remarkable men and learning from them about the struggles they face—struggles that in many ways are not so different from the struggles I face as a woman.

This question came from a teenager. It is definitely true that teenaged men aren't as visibly "emotional" as teenaged women. (*No one* is as visibly emotional as teenaged women. I remember once as a teenager crying for an entire *day*, and nothing was even wrong. It's a hormone thing.) But because men don't *show* their emotions the way women do, we assume they don't *have* them. And that is wrong.

Emotions are good. They were created by God to be signposts for our psychological health. *Everyone* has them. Some people may carry their emotions closer to the surface, while others may have been suppressing their feelings for so long that they are not sure where to find them anymore. But they are in there—always.

The thing is, God made women and men differently. (I'll bet you already knew that.) He not only made us different physically, He made us different *emotionally*. We tend to live and express our emotions in different ways.

Women tend to talk about their feelings—and talk, and talk, and talk. When I am upset, there is nothing more important to me than finding a good friend (or nine good friends—it doesn't matter) and talking the whole thing out, viewing it from several different angles and basically wallowing in the whole situation for a while. Men, on the other hand, tend to want to be by themselves and think through their problems. They don't tend to share their problems until they are ready to solve them.

This behavior tends to lead to the assumption that relationships don't mean as much to men, and they are not as hurt when a relationship ends. I *know* that is false—I speak to men all the time who are absolutely devastated by the breakup of a relationship. In fact, studies show that, on the whole, it takes men far *longer* to get over relationships than it takes women.

People think that breakups are harder on women because they are often more visibly upset at the end of a relationship. They cry and mourn and talk to their friends for hours on end. But this is exactly why they tend to heal sooner. They get their pain out into the open. They reach out for help. They *deal* with it. That brings quicker healing.

Men, on the other hand, are more inclined to try to face their pain alone. To compound that tendency, they often face a certain "macho" stereotype in society. They are expected to be "strong and silent". They are not *supposed* to fall apart at the end of a relationship. Combine that expectation with the fact that men are not as verbal as women, and we should not be surprised that men tend to keep more inside. They don't talk as much about their pain or their problems. That, however, is bad. Pain kept inside tends to fester. It gets worse. It is much more difficult to deal with problems that are never aired.

To answer the question: Men *are* emotional. Some men are more emotional than others, just as some women are more emotional than others. But I believe that most men love very deeply and hurt very deeply when they lose love. Because they are wired differently from the way women are, however, they don't express their love or their pain in exactly the same way women do. They may not express that pain. But that doesn't mean it is not there.

I speak as a woman. But I hope I speak for at least some of you men out there. I may not have felt your pain, but I have seen it. I have seen it in your letters and in those of you who come up to me after a talk, sharing with me your devastation over the loss of a love, or your intense love, dedication and concern for a friend, a family member or a woman. I know you guys are out there. And I think you are all very, very wonderful.

Women, don't be so quick to judge men. Just because he isn't talking about it doesn't mean he isn't hurting. And men, remember that admitting you are in pain is not the worst thing that could happen. In fact, talking it out could be among the best things you could do.

"Why is it women seem emotionally unstable at times?"

Here is a male's version of the previous question. Why do the women he sees get so upset sometimes? Why do they cry so much? Why are their emotions always so, well, *there,* while men are usually so much calmer?

There are several reasons for this discrepancy, some of which we have touched upon already. First, especially for teenaged women, there is the hormonal factor. The teenage years are a time of serious hormonal upheaval. The hormonal and reproductive systems are still developing. Hormone levels vacillate wildly. These hormones can play absolute havoc with a woman's emotional state. Women, especially teenaged or pregnant women, often react very emotionally to relatively minor situations or even when there is nothing whatsoever to be upset about. People around them may not like it, and may tell them to "pull themselves together", but that is more easily said than done. Women don't like crying for no reason any more than others like to listen to them.

The second reason, as we discussed above, is that women as a rule express their feelings more than men do. Studies consistently show that women are more verbal than men, speaking up to ten times more words than their male counterparts every day. Therefore, they are more likely to talk about their feelings. Men, as we discussed, seem to be more likely to keep those feelings inside.

Showing or expressing emotion is not in itself a sign of "emotional instability". In fact, identifying and expressing emotion can often be the healthiest thing to do. Feelings are neither bad nor good in themselves. They are signs. Our job is to examine them, to understand where they come from, to control their expression, and to deal with the situation or situations that brought the feelings about.

If someone is feeling and expressing an emotion, it does very little good to say, "Don't feel that way." The feeling is there, and it won't go away just because it is told to do so. The feeling must be examined and dealt with.

Feelings need to be taken seriously, but that doesn't give us license to express them any way we choose. This is particularly true when it comes to anger. Angry feelings come from *somewhere*—frustration, insecurity, maybe even righteous indignation. But taking that anger out on another person is never right. The best thing to do is to work the anger off in some kind of neutral context (running, chopping wood, biting nails in half, whatever) and *then* deal with the situation and try to figure out where the anger is coming from.

If you are with someone who is sad or crying, the best thing to do is to let him or her "let it all out". Crying does help. A friend of mine recently lost his wife to cancer. He told me, "She used to tell me it was okay to cry—that she felt better after she cried. I always thought, 'That's dumb. After you cry you feel worse.' Now I know she was right. I cry a lot these days."

None of this is to say that a certain individual may or may

not be emotionally unstable. Certainly there are enough factors in modern society that could lead to an individual, male or female, being to some extent emotionally unstable. In this case, again, the solution is not just to repress the emotions but to put the person in contact with a Christian professional who can assist in sorting through the emotions and getting to the root of the problem.

Sexual Peak

"Define sexual peak."

First of all, let's talk about what sexual peak *isn't*. Sexual peak is not a reference to any certain age when sex is "best" or most enjoyable. We have already seen that studies show that the "best" sex is sex between happily married people —of any age.

The term "sexual peak" simply refers to the age at which a person is the most easily aroused sexually. Because men and women have different hormonal systems and different developmental "timetables", sexual peak for men is different from what it is for women.

Sexual peak for males, according to most of the literature I have read, happens at about the age of eighteen. This means that eighteen-year-old males are more easily aroused than they will probably be at any other time in their lives. This doesn't mean that sex is "best" for them at that age. In fact, being too easily aroused is most likely to have the opposite effect.

Females, on the other hand, don't reach their sexual peak until about age thirty-five—almost twice the age of the male's sexual peak.

Do you see the potential for trouble here? Say there are two teenagers in a car. She is scheduled to reach her sexual peak in about nineteen years. He is scheduled to reach his sexual peak . . . right about now. She is probably enjoying all the cuddling and closeness and is still quite easily able to control herself. Meanwhile, he is having a very different kind of reaction.

It's very important, in the course of affectionate dating behavior, to understand that men and women are not sexually "wired" in the same way. Teenaged men tend to be much more easily aroused. As women get older, the balance changes. It is important to understand, however, that even though you may be reacting or responding in a certain way, your date may be reacting in a very different way.

"Do men have a hard time with their hormones when they are around women, and why don't women usually have this problem?"

"Why does chastity always seem to refer to the female sex?"

"Why does it seem like guys have no control, and girls are always the ones to say 'no'?"

Again, sexual peak and differences in wiring account for some differences here.

I placed these questions in a separate section, however, because I wanted to make a specific point. Women are often told that they have a responsibility to keep things under control. This is because it is assumed that the female half of the couple may be less aroused than the male and more easily able to stop affection before it goes out of control. There is some truth to this argument.

It is, however, absolutely, categorically incorrect to say that the responsibility for maintaining chastity rests with the woman alone. This should not be seen as a license for men just to "abdicate" their moral responsibility. Men of a certain age may have a stronger sex drive overall, but that does not mean that they cannot, or should not, control that sex drive. In fact, on the contrary, if they are more easily tempted, then they should be particularly vigilant about getting into tempting situations.

If a man is on a date, he is responsible not only for maintaining his own purity but for protecting the purity of his date. The same goes for his date. They each need to take responsibility for themselves as well as to make an effort to protect each other. And they need to take that responsibility seriously. Each needs to be willing and able to say "no" if necessary.

Teasing

"Will a guy think badly of a woman if she messes around without having any intention of sleeping with him?"

Maybe. "Messing around" without any intention of having sex is not a very nice thing to do to someone. It is like saying, "I love you so much I am going to make you want something, and then I am not going to give it to you."

That said, I want to make something else clear. Just because you may have "messed around" and gone farther than you should have does not mean you should keep going because you have made someone want sex.

Let me repeat that. *It is wrong to have sex just because you have "turned someone on"*. Arousal goes away. It has never killed anyone. Going "all the way" out of pity has, however, killed many people and ruined a lot of lives.

The correct thing to do when you realize you have "gone too far" is to stop immediately, apologize and either go to a public place or go home. Period.

"Does He Like Me?"

"If you go out on a date with a guy and you kiss and stuff, how do you know if the guy is initiating it because he likes you?"

You don't know. That's why "kissing and stuff" is not the best way to gauge someone's feelings for you.

The old song goes "If you want to know if he loves you so, it's in his kiss." I disagree. If you want to know if he loves you, look at how he treats you. Look at the respect he shows you. Look at whether or not he respects your purity. Look at whether his primary concern is his own selfish desires or what is best for you.

Men Who Respect Sex and the Women Who Love Them

"Do you think it's fair that a majority of guys out there have had sex?"

I don't necessarily think it's true. Look at this society. Virginity, and especially male virginity, is not exactly valued. The unfortunate male tradition of bragging about sexual conquests has been around for a long time. Very few guys are going to pipe up in the locker room to announce that they are virgins. But that doesn't mean that none of them is. I personally know of several attractive red-blooded males who are still virgins in their thirties.

"Why don't men perceive sex as something sacred and intimately shared between a man and a woman as most women do?"

It is impossible to say that "men" respect sex or they don't. There are billions of men in the world. Some are wonderful, caring guys. Some are selfish users. For that matter, some women are loving women while others are manipulators or gold diggers.

My experience has been that there are many, many terrific men in the world, men who respect women and respect sex. Men, strive to be a man like that. Women, strive to date men like that and to be the kind of woman who deserves them.

"Do all guys think girls are just a way for them to get sex?"

No. Hold out for one who doesn't, and avoid the others like the plague.

Men Who Lie about Sex

"Why do guys lie about having sex with a bunch of girls?"

Because those particular guys are selfish, egocentric jerks. There are too many wonderful men in the world to waste your time on guys like this. Stay away from them, and remember that no one with any brains believes them anyway.

"Why is it that a guy will pressure you for sex, then call you a slut after you've done it?"

See the above answer. This is a particularly cruel thing to do to a girl, but unfortunately I have talked to far too many girls who have experienced it. This is why it is very important not to give in to pressure to have sex in the first place. Sex is clearly not a way to "make" someone love you. Instead, it equips him with a powerful ability to hurt you later on.

Second, if you have made a mistake, it is important to seek forgiveness from God, to seek your strength and your confidence from Him and to ignore as much as possible the meaningless taunts of a petty, mean-spirited jerk.

"Why Don't They Treat Us Better?"

"Why do women treat guys so badly?"

"Why do so many guys use girls?"

People, especially dates, treat you badly for one reason and one reason alone—because you let them. Every time your girlfriend or boyfriend uses or abuses you and you stay around, you are sending a message: "You can get away with this and still keep me. I won't leave."

Whining doesn't work. "Please don't treat me badly" doesn't work. The best thing you can do for that person and for yourself is to show him or her the consequences of treating someone badly—the person leaves. Don't leave to teach her a lesson or to change him. Leave because it's the best thing for you to do. Leave because it frees you to find someone who *really* loves you. Leave now because staying won't solve anything, and if you marry someone like this, leaving may no longer be such a simple option.

The jerks of the world will change only when being a jerk doesn't work anymore. When no one will put up with mean-spiritedness, manipulation and abusiveness, then mean-spirited, manipulative and abusive people will find themselves alone. Then maybe they'll get the message. In the meantime, if you put up with it, you are a part of the problem.

Women—What Do They Want in a Man?

"What do women most want in men?"

We don't want just what you think we want—a good-looking guy with a great body who drives a Porsche.

It may sound like a cliché, but most women want a man who loves her and respects her and treasures her; someone who will be trustworthy and who will be a dedicated husband and father. She wants emotional intimacy and companionship and support. She wants someone who is emotionally healthy and who won't flake out when times get tough. She wants someone who loves *her* in particular, not just women in general. She wants a loving, lifetime partner.

See? None of that has anything to do with a Porsche. . . .

10

Single Survival

Dating

"Why was dating invented, anyway?"

Here is a question I have asked myself a couple of times.

Whoever invented dating did not design it as a way to torture single people. Nor is dating supposed to be a way for you to get your USRDA of love and romance.

Dating is about finding a marriage partner. That's all. Of course, if you're younger, you may be just trying to figure out the opposite sex in general, and you're probably not looking at marriage in the immediate future, but that doesn't change the fact that marriage is the long-term goal of dating.

"Why is it that if a girl goes out with more than one guy, people look down on her?"

It is my personal opinion that the entire institution of dating is a little messed up these days.

I was not around in the 1950s, but from what I have heard, people handled dating a little bit differently. They seemed to recognize that dating is about getting to know people. If you wanted to get to know someone, you went on a date. If you both wanted to get to know each other better, you went on more dates. If, in the meantime, there was someone *else* you wanted to get to know, you could go on a date with that person also. "Going steady", as it was called back then, was a big step. Agreeing not to date others was generally accepted as an indication that a couple was seriously considering marriage. But as long as you had not taken that step, there was nothing socially unacceptable about dating several different people at the same time.

Try that today and see what kind of names people call you.

What happened to change things? Sex. It is no big deal to go to dinner and a movie with someone and then hear that he had dinner and a movie with someone else. It *is* a big deal, however, to go to bed with someone and then hear that he went to bed with someone else. We are not *made* to share our sexual partners. Sex speaks a permanent, exclusive language. Sex says, "You and only you", not "you and my date next Saturday and anyone else I happen to meet in the meantime."

Once sex outside marriage became acceptable, dating changed radically. This permanent bond began to enter temporary dating relationships, and those relationships became much more intense, unstable and painful. Dating at that point became much more monogamous—or at least there was an *expectation* that dating would be monogamous. People who were dating several people at the same time were assumed to be *sleeping* with several different people, and that still is not considered socially (or morally) acceptable. As soon as a couple had been on two or three dates, it was generally assumed that they would no longer date others.

The fifties may not have been perfect, but I believe we should return to a dating system that in some ways resembles their system. Dating *should* be about getting to know members of the opposite sex. There should be nothing wrong with going on dates with several different people. Every time you accept a date with someone, it should not mean that you *can't* date anyone else in the foreseeable future. "Going steady" *should* be a big deal. It should imply that a couple is seriously considering marriage. It should not just be some kind of "artificial marriage", taking you out of circulation, tying you down to someone you probably won't marry and guaranteeing a painful breakup down the line.

Of course, if we were going to return to a system like that of the fifties, we would need to make some other changes. There could not be sexual activity in dating. You cannot date multiple people and still engage in sexual activity on those dates. That would not be dating; it would be promiscuity. Dating would have to be about talking and getting to know each other, not about having sex or making out or getting "hot and bothered" in the back seat of a car. Affection in this kind of dating would have to be limited to hugs and light kisses.

To return to a system like this would also mean that dating would not be a good place to "find love" in the short run. If you believe that every new date is someone who will cure your loneliness and love you unconditionally, this kind of system won't work for you. Of course, no system *will* work for you. A date *can't* love you unconditionally at this point. Dating is conditional—by definition. It is about dating and rejecting a lot of different people until you find one with whom you want to spend the rest of your life. In the meantime, your needs for love, support and companionship must be met elsewhere—by friends, family and community. Those are the people who will stay around for the long run.

Until there is a ring on your finger, you should not be relying on dates for love, or for anything but respectful treatment and pleasant conversation. While you are dating, you should be able to enjoy that respectful treatment and pleasant conversation with several different people.

"If you make a date with one girl at one time, then before the time of the date you meet another girl and she asks you out for the same night and you'd rather go out with the second, what should you do?"

Go out with the first. If girl number two is interested in you, she will understand. If she is mature at all, she will respect you more for keeping your word to girl number one. She will still be around tomorrow.

"What is a good thing to do on a first date?"

On a first date, do anything that is fun and lets you get to know each other better. Plan something where you will be *doing* something, so that you will have something to keep you busy and to talk about during the date. Go rollerblading, or putt-putt golfing, or biking, or whatever sounds like fun to you. If you are going to a movie, go to dinner first, so you will have a chance to talk and get to know each other.[1]

If you are taking a woman out for the first time, pay for any expenses. If you continue to date, there will be plenty of time for her to do nice things for you later. This is your turn. Whatever you do doesn't have to cost a lot of money. Be creative. If you need help with ideas, there is a book called *Creative Dating*[2] that could give you some.

Whatever you do, plan *something*. Don't pick her up and then do the "What do you want to do?" "I don't know, what do you want to do?" thing. That is the kiss of death for a date.

Flirting

"Is it bad to flirt?"

If by "flirt" you mean "express sincere interest in the opposite sex", then no, it is not bad to flirt at all. This is how men and women throughout the ages have indicated interest in each other.

---

[1] If you're going to a movie, also make sure the movie you choose has no sex scenes. There is nothing more horrifying than sitting with someone you barely know, watching enormous, naked people doing embarrassingly private things.

[2] Doug Fields and Todd Temple, *Creative Dating* (Nashville: Oliver Nelson Publishers, 1986).

If, on the other hand, you mean "get an ego boost by attracting the attention of someone I'm not interested in", then flirting can be cruel. To pretend you are interested in someone you are *not* particularly interested in, just as a way of boosting your ego or entertaining yourself, is using another person, and it is wrong.

The "Perfect" Partner?

"Do you think you will ever know if you find the 'perfect' man or woman?"

No one is perfect. This, unfortunately, has been true ever since Adam ate the apple. You will never find a partner who is perfectly smart, or perfectly romantic, or perfectly anything.

This does not, however, mean that you should settle for the first person who comes along. Some people are far more perfect than others, and some are more perfect for *you* than others.

I have always said that there are deep flaws and there are surface flaws. Surface flaws may include having a strange laugh, failing to put the toilet seat up or down, preferring American cars to Japanese, or vice versa, and so on. These are flaws that, if you can live with them, are no big deal. Deep-down flaws, on the other hand, include a violent temper, physical or emotional abusiveness, an interest in pornography, dishonesty, drug or alcohol addiction, or unfaithfulness. These are traits that should make you run away—and run fast.

"I'll Change Him!"

"I'm seeing this guy. I know he is not perfect by a long shot, but I really think I can change him."

Banish those words from your vocabulary!!

The words "I'll change him" have caused more pain and heartbreak than any other words in the history of men and women.

If you want to change the way he dresses, fine. If you want to change his eating habits, that's okay, too. If, however, you think you are going to take a liar, or an abuser, or a cheat, and turn him into Mr. Model Husband of the Year, you have a big surprise coming. It won't be nice.

People lie or cheat or abuse because (a) they have deep, significant emotional problems; (b) they are selfish, insensitive jerks; or (c) both. Either way, you can't help. You are not a therapist, and you are not a miracle worker. Meanwhile, staying with someone like that will chip away at *your* self-respect and security until *you* need a therapist, too. Believe me, I have seen it over and over again.

I realize that single Christians of all ages are particularly prone to this. It is part of our loving, helping nature. We want to do unto others, but we often get carried away. Helping people who want help is nice. It is not, however, a good idea to date them. Dating is about finding someone who already *has* his or her act together—not about "remodeling" someone.

Some people *like* being in a relationship with someone who needs help. This is called "co-dependency". It means that they "need" to be "needed", and it is not healthy. Co-dependents will let their own lives, jobs or schoolwork all slide in their efforts to "help" this other person. Healthy relationships are not supposed to work that way. Good relationships are supposed to be good for you. They are supposed to make you feel better. They are supposed to make you happier and more productive.

It's fine to want to help people who need help. But *please* don't date them. If you constantly find yourself attracted to dishonest, abusive or emotionally unstable people, try to figure out why. Make a couple of appointments with a good Christian therapist. Work through whatever issues cause this attraction. But don't, *don't* keep dating losers or emotionally unstable people. Save your dates for healthy people.

"What is a good age to get married?"

Again, there are no hard and fast rules. I do know, as we said earlier, that the time from ages sixteen to twenty-one are years of tremendous growth and change. Marrying before twenty-one can often be risky. You are not through maturing, and it is easy to "outgrow" someone at this stage of development.

Beyond this, it is hard to say. Everyone is different. I do know this: You should not marry until you have accomplished all you want or need to accomplish as a single person. If you want to study in Europe or volunteer as a missionary, do it. This is your best chance. Once you are married, you will have responsibilities that take away your freedom to do as you please.

I think it is particularly important for a young woman to live on her own and support herself before getting married. Far too many women go straight from being supported by Daddy or Mommy to being supported by a husband. This is extremely unhealthy. You need to have the confidence of knowing that you can take care of yourself. If something were to happen to your husband, you would have to take care of yourself and your family. This is not a possibility to dismiss or take lightly. When you have children, you take responsibility for them, and you need to know that you could handle it alone, if necessary.

I personally think it is a good idea to spend some good quality single time before rushing into marriage. Being single allows you opportunities to travel, study, learn and live in ways no longer available to you after you marry. All of the learning, traveling and studying you do will help you to be a better spouse and parent. Far too many people rush into marriage at a young age and then regret missing out on opportunities they could have had if they had waited a few more years to marry.

All of that being said, there is one and only one "right" time to get married—when you find and fall in love with someone with whom you want to share your children as well as the rest of your life. This is no short order. Your head and your heart need to agree. You need to *know* that this person is responsible, selfless and loving, and to *feel* enthusiastic about waking up with this person every single day for the rest of your life.

This, and only this, is the reason to get married. Don't get married because you have reached a certain age and you are afraid that if you don't get married now you never will. Don't get married because you want to have a pretty wedding with lots of bridesmaids. Don't get married because you want to have sex. Don't get married because someone asked, and you are afraid no one will ever ask again.

Marry in haste, repent in leisure.

Healthy Relationships

"How do you know when you have found a good relationship?"

You know you have found a good relationship when you are with someone you trust completely; someone who trusts you completely; someone who shares your faith in God; someone who treats you as the image and likeness of God that you are; someone who puts what is best for you ahead of his own selfish desires; someone who allows you the freedom to do whatever you need to do to grow and mature, even if it means spending a lot of time apart; someone who encourages you to make and maintain other friendships; someone to whom you can tell your deepest, darkest secrets; someone to whom you can always turn whether you are happy or sad; someone you enjoy being with; someone with whom you can work out differences constructively; and someone you would like your children to resemble.

Sound like a tall order? It is, but such a person exists. This is a description of a mature, loving person. Hold out for one.

"How do females relate to relationships differently?"

I sometimes ask teenaged men and women to do an exercise where they write two lists. First they list the traits of their ideal date. Then they list the traits of their ideal mate. It is interesting—the results never vary. For the women, the two lists are almost identical. In looking for dates for this weekend, they are seeking the same traits they seek in a husband. For men, the lists are very different. What they look for in a date is often not at all what they would look for in a wife.

This says something significant about the different approaches young men and women take to dating. Women take it much more seriously. They are beginning the search for "happily ever after". Men, on the other hand, are not so interested in the long run at this point in their lives.

I suppose this should not be surprising. Men often feel they have a lot to do before they get married. The burden of being a breadwinner for the family is usually placed primarily on them. To do that well, they need several years of school and/or professional experience. It is okay not to be in any rush to get married before they are prepared to take on the responsibilities.

It is not necessary to change this situation, but we do need to understand it. Teenage men tend to be more casual about dating. Teenage women need to respect that, and not expect some overarching commitment from every guy they date in high school. Likewise, guys should realize that women take dating seriously, and these men should not "tease" these women or give them the impression they are more serious than they are. A little honesty goes a long way.

By the time men and women reach their early to mid-twenties, this situation evens out a little. A lot of people say that women are more interested in marriage than men are, but I believe this is a stereotype. More mature people often tend to be more interested and ready for marriage than immature people, male or female. Of course, immature people are also sometimes interested in marriage as a way to escape their problems or to cure loneliness, but this again applies to both males and females.

It is true that women think and talk about relationships more than men do. One look at a woman's choices in magazines proves this to be true. *Popular Mechanics* and *GQ* never have articles with titles like "Does She Really Like You? Ten Ways to Tell" or "Quiz: Rating Your Kissability". This is not because men don't care whether or not women are interested in them, but rather because (a) they don't think about their relationships all of the time, and (b) they wouldn't be caught dead reading about it in a magazine. Men often prefer to focus their attention on *things* —things they can fix or change or manipulate. They like to read about cars and boats and computers and airplanes.

None of this means that men are not interested in relationships. They just don't dwell on the subject for days and weeks on end the way women tend to do.

"Do you believe in interracial relationships?"

I have no problem whatsoever with interracial relationships. I don't care if people are white, black, brown or even green, as long as they really love each other, respect each other and put God first in their relationship.

I think that many people opposed interracial relationships in the past because they were concerned that, if the couple married, their mixed-race children would suffer or be considered outcasts. That may have been true in previous generations, but I don't think it is true to any significant extent today—at least not where I have lived. There are a *lot* of mixed-race kids, especially in San Francisco. It has almost become the norm. I think that is a very good thing.

Depending on the people and the races involved, interracial relationships can be *difficult*. There may be cultural differences to overcome, and that can put pressure on a relationship. That alone may cause some parents to be concerned when one of their children begins to date someone of another race. But as I said, I think the problems vary with individuals and cultures. Some people can handle it, some can't.

Of course, some people oppose interracial relationships for other reasons—bigotry, racism, a desire for some kind of "racial purity". I think that kind of attitude is ridiculous. There is no reason to dignify it with a response.

Too Busy to Date

"I don't have time to date. Will this affect my future dating?"

Not at all. You just keep right on being busy, developing your talents and becoming the best person you can. When you feel ready to explore serious relationships with the opposite sex, you will make the time.

I do believe that it is important is to have good, close, platonic *friendships* with people of the opposite sex. You need to know how to relate to them, how they are different from you as well as ways in which they are similar. There is no better way to do that than in the safety of a good, emotionally intimate friendship. That way, when you do start to date, it won't feel like stepping onto another planet or anything. You will already be somewhat familiar with the territory.

Opposite-Sex Friends

"What if you have a guy friend, and he is nice, but you are not attracted to him?"

There are two possibilities here. One is that he is not attracted to you either. In that case, you have a very good thing—a platonic relationship with a man who can give you the "inside view" of a guy's mind. He can help you to understand how men are emotionally different from women. I have had several "buddies" like that, and they are real treasures in my life.

The other possibility, and I suspect this is the source of your question, is that he *is* attracted to you. This is a little more complicated. For suggestions on how to handle the situation, read the next two questions.

"Is platonic love possible when only one person wants more? Would it be difficult? Would affection be misinterpreted?"

This is a tough question. The answer depends on the two people involved and the intensity of feelings on the part of the person who wants more. On the whole, one-sided friendships like this tend to be very painful for the person who feels stronger. In the end, these friendships tend to self-destruct.

If you are the person who just wants to be friends, remember that you have tremendous power to hurt this person. Make sure that your intentions toward the relationship are clear. And make sure that you act consistently. *Never* lead this person on. Don't act as you would with a date. Don't "use" this person for affection or to have a date when you are desperate.

If you are the person who wants more, face reality. After you have known each other for a certain period of time, either there is mutual love or there is not. Don't keep hanging around, hoping that somehow your friend will suddenly "see the light" and everything will change. It probably won't happen. Get on with your life. Free yourself to find someone who loves you.

It would be easy to say that when the pain gets too bad, the person who wants more will eventually face reality. But some people are gluttons for punishment. There is a certain safety in sticking around someone you know well. Hoping this person's mind will change seems easier than taking a risk with someone new. In the long run, however, this just leads to more pain and pressure. In the end, it can ruin whatever was left of what may have started as a good friendship.

"How can a woman just be friends with a guy without leading him on?"

Very carefully.

Make clear boundaries from the beginning. Make it clear that you see this relationship as a treasured friendship but nothing more. Then act that way.

I know it is easy, when a single woman has a male friend, sometimes to rely on him as a standby "date" or to turn to him when she wants male affection or attention. That is using him. Don't do it. Resist the temptation. Don't treat him like a "date". Don't "flirt" with him or joke around about falling in love with him or marrying him if there is *any* possibility he may take it seriously. Don't be physically affectionate with him in the way you would with a date. Don't monopolize his time so that he never spends time with other women. Don't act jealous or possessive.

Platonic friends are a treasure. Don't mistreat them or take them for granted.

Falling in Love with a Friend

"Can sincere friendships turn into a serious relationship?"

Yes, they can. Sometimes the best dating relationships start out as friendships. I know that has been the case for me.

It is a lot easier to get to know someone as a friend. There is not any "first date" pressure. You can relax and be yourself, knowing that you don't have to impress this person or decide right now whether or not you want a long-term relationship with this person.

C. S. Lewis says that friends stand side by side looking out at the world while lovers stand face to face, looking at each other. And often, in the course of a male-female friendship, two people cease looking out at the world and begin to turn toward each other. They begin to see each other differently. They discover deeper qualities in the other person, qualities that may not have been so readily apparent in a dating situation, where both parties are nervous and putting on a little bit of an act. They begin to develop real emotional intimacy. They grow closer, and often they fall in love. Some of the best, most solid marriages begin as friendships. After all, marriage partners are lovers and partners, but they are also, essentially, friends. Marriage is a very deep, abiding, permanent friendship. What better way to start?

That being said, it is also true that some people *mistake* friendship for love. They begin to develop a sexual attraction toward a friend of the opposite sex and mistake this for love. This is not love. Sexual attraction is a normal phenomenon between males and females, but it doesn't necessarily indicate the presence of real love. Real love means wanting to make this person your partner for life—seeing him as the best possible person to wake up with in the morning, to raise your children and to lead you to heaven. Just because a friend is comfortable to be around, or you are easily able to share secrets or you are sexually attracted to each other, you are not necessarily in love, and you should not get seriously involved or marry on that basis alone.

"Will becoming 'romantically involved' necessarily ruin a friendship?"

Well, I guarantee it will never be the same again.

As I said, most of my best dating relationships have started out as friendships. Most of those men are still my friends today—friends I treasure very much. But our friendships are not the *same* as they were before we started dating. And after we broke up, it took quite a while to rebuild any friendship at all.

Becoming "romantically involved" with anyone involves a risk. There are only two possible outcomes. You will either get married or you will break up.[3] If you eventually break up, there is guaranteed to be a certain amount of pain involved, and rebuilding a friendship is not always easy, or even possible. Either way, things will never, ever be the same. That is why a romantic relationship should not be entered into lightly.

There are situations where it is good to move from friendship to a more serious relationship. If you are both sincerely interested in exploring the possibility of some day marrying each other, and if your feelings for each other in that regard have become strong, there is no sense "pretending"

---

[3] An audience member once suggested a third potential outcome, but we're not considering the possibility of death right now.

to be no more than friends. That would be attempting to shove the relationship into a space it no longer fits, and it doesn't work for long.

If you are exploring this possibility with a friend, move carefully. The stakes are high, but there can be real rewards. I know I have never regretted it.

"How do you make the jump from friendship to dating?"

Again, very carefully. If you have had an honest relationship from the start, making this jump should be much easier.

If your feelings for a friend change, and you suspect that his or her feelings have changed too, you are going to need to discuss it sooner or later. I know it can be scary to make yourself vulnerable like that, but the only other option is to wait in uncertainty and play guessing games. If he or she is not interested in changing the friendship, then finding out early will hurt in the short run, but it will save you months and maybe years of hoping for something that will never happen.

If you both agree you'd like to move forward, then congratulations! Move slowly, be careful to respect each other sexually, continue to respect each other's freedom, and enjoy your new relationship!

Breaking Up

"How do you know when you should break up with someone?"

Every situation is different, of course, so it is impossible to give an exact answer. There are, however, a few situations where I would say a breakup is *definitely* in order.

1. *Certainty that you will not marry:* Dating is about figuring out if you want to spend the rest of your life with someone. If, in the course of dating this person, you conclude that he is definitely not the one you want, then it is time to get out.

It is not fair, to you or to the other person, to stay in a relationship past this point. If you want to marry, you will *have* to break up eventually, in order to find the person you will marry. In stalling, you are only prolonging the inevitable.

Maybe he is a nice guy. Maybe she is wonderful. But that doesn't mean this is the right person for *you*. Don't stick around trying to talk yourself into staying with someone if you know, deep in your heart, that this is not the right one.

I know it is easy to want to stick around—for security, for companionship, for affection. It is not fair, however, to you or to the other person. If marriage is your goal, this relationship is taking both of you out of circulation. Maybe the one you *should* marry is just around the corner. But if you are still hanging around with Mr. or Ms. Nowhere Relationship, you are going to miss out.

2. *Habitual dishonesty:* Does this person lie to you? This is not good.

Good relationships are based on trust. It is impossible to build a relationship without that trust. You cannot rely on someone, give your life to someone or share children with someone if you can't even be sure that what is coming out of that person's mouth is in fact true. The entire foundation of the relationship is gone.

If someone lies, there is a reason. That person doesn't want you to know something. Whether it is about what he is doing, or where she has been, or maybe a secret from the past, you need to know about it. You can't make decisions about the relationship if you don't have the whole picture. And he or she would not keep the whole picture from you for no reason. Where there is smoke, there is often fire.

Don't make excuses for this person, and don't buy into "it's none of my business." A lie is a lie is a lie. Unless it is about a surprise party or your Christmas present, a lie has no place in your relationship.

3. *Pornography:* If he is into pornography, he is not into you. At least not the way he should be.

Throwing it away is not enough. There are probably a lifetime of images already burned onto his brain—images that will get in the way of a healthy marital sexual relationship. Stick around only if you see true repentance and a consistent new attitude of chastity.

4. *Drug use or alcoholism:* These substances radically alter a person's personality and behavior. I don't care how nice

she is when she is straight. You need more stability and predictability than this person can offer.

"But", you are crying, *"he needs me. I can help."* I know. I have been there. I have cried the same cry. Guess what? You can't help. He needs a lot more help than you can give.

You're not the Betty Ford Clinic. Don't try to be.

5. *Illegal activities:* This should speak for itself. Say "adios", or we'll have to start calling you Clyde—or maybe Bonnie.

6. *Abusiveness:* If you are dating someone who has been either physically or emotionally abusive to you, get out. If anyone hits you, shoves you or in any other way threatens your physical safety, this is no one you want to be with. The same goes for someone who consistently insults you, demeans you or calls you names. This is not appropriate behavior, and it is a symptom of a much deeper disorder.

I don't care if it happened just once. I don't care how sorry he is. I don't care if there is a long apology letter and a heartfelt commitment to change. If someone "loves" you and yet is able to abuse you, he has a serious problem that runs much, much deeper than what you have seen. The time to find that out is now—not after the ring is on the finger.

This person may be very sincere. He or she may be very sorry. But only the grace of God and intensive therapy will address whatever issues brought on the abusiveness in the first place. Christian therapy is where this person should be. Even then, you should not stick around waiting for therapy to work. You should not go back unless a competent therapist can assure you that the problem has been *completely* eradicated and that he is no longer a threat. Don't put your life on hold in the meantime—that could take years, if it happens at all. Even then, I would be extremely wary.

7. *Control:* Does he always demand to know where you are or what you have been doing? Does she keep you from pursuing outside interests, hobbies or friendships? Does he demand all of your time or attention? Does this relationship keep you from being free to make decisions about your life?

If this is the case, get out. You are not this person's property. You are your own, autonomous person. You need to grow, to live and to make decisions. No one should keep you from doing that, especially someone who supposedly loves you.

8. *Excessive turmoil in your life:* I once heard a song with the line: "For every time that we spent laughing there were two times that I cried." Is that your relationship? If so, think twice.

I know—you have got such wonderful memories, and there *was* that occasional time you spent laughing, but look at the whole picture. Is this relationship making our overall life better or worse? If it is worse, do you want the *rest* of your life to look like this? Marriage can be difficult, to be sure, but on the whole it is supposed to make your life *better*, not worse. Any problems you have before marriage will still be there, and probably worse, after you marry.

"When spouses or boyfriends/girlfriends cheat on their partners why is it that we often do not blame them but the person they are cheating with?"

It can be difficult to accept that someone we believed loved us could cheat on us. It becomes far easier instead to blame the other person. But, as the old saying goes, "It takes two to tango." If someone cheated on you, it was not because there was a gun pointed at his head. It is time to wake up and take a good look at reality. A person who cheats once is likely to cheat again. It is time to get out while you still can—*before* the ring is on the finger.

"How do you dump an irritating, two-timing loser?"

Very quickly.

No one ever teaches us how to break up with someone. Most of us are left to figure it out on our own. But given the fact that dating is about weeding through lots of people to find one to marry, it is important to be able to get out of a dead-end relationship honestly and gracefully.

Make your decision and stick with it. If you think it is time to break up with someone, think about your decision very carefully. Don't just do it to lash out in the heat of an argument and then go back when you have cooled off. Think it through, and make sure it is what you want to do.

Once you have made your decision, don't, repeat, *don't* just stop calling. This is very cruel. If you were in any kind of dating relationship, it is not fair just to suddenly disappear from someone's life. Everyone deserves an explanation.

You need to talk to this person, and you need to do it soon. I know it is easy to stall, sometimes for months. It is difficult to hurt someone. But staying around when it is not right is not doing that person any favor, either. It doesn't take a genius to figure out when someone is not happy in a relationship. He may have already caught on.

When you talk, be honest. Again, it is easy to try to say only as much as you have to in order to get out, but that is not fair. That person deserves to know exactly why you are leaving. Otherwise it is impossible to process what has happened and learn from it. The only thing worse than being dumped is being dumped without understanding the reason.

Be kind. This is not the time to get angry or assess blame. If this person has been dishonest or abusive, then saying just that—honestly and calmly—speaks more than angry rages or crying fits ever could.

Stick to your decision. It is easy to feel lonely after a breakup. It is perfectly normal suddenly to remember all the great times and forget about the bad. It happens to everyone. It will happen to you. Expect it, and don't give in to the temptation to call her, or to write him a note to share the memory or look for comfort or "just to talk". It is a mistake.

"When I break up with my girlfriend, do I have to stop speaking to her?"

I honestly believe that couples who break up need to be completely apart for a time. How long that time is depends on who they are, what the relationship was like and why they broke up.

I broke up with my high-school boyfriend . . . well, too many times, over the course of several years. Every time we broke up, we would end up calling each other, trying to be "friends", and eventually going right back into a relationship that never seemed to work. The last time we broke up, he asked me never to call him again. He said he wanted to get on with his life. I was upset. We had spent a lot of years together. There was a lot of history between us. We were very close. As painful as the relationship had been, I could not imagine the thought of never speaking to him again.

But I respected his wishes. It wasn't easy at first. But after a few months, I came to realize that this was the best thing that could have happened. We weren't right for each other, but as long as we kept popping into each others' lives, we prevented each other from moving on. It was only in breaking up all the way that we were both able finally to get on with our lives.

I have already said this several times, but it bears repeating here. There is good pain, and there is bad pain. Good pain is like the pain you experience with exercise. It hurts, but there is a reason. You are getting stronger. Something good is happening. Bad pain is like the pain of a broken bone or cancer. There is nothing good about it. It is there because something is very wrong, and it just keeps on hurting. The only way to get rid of the pain is through giving in to some good pain, like setting the bone or having surgery.

It is bad pain to keep going back to a relationship over

and over again, because it represents security or because it is easier to go back than it is to start to date again. It is good pain to want desperately to call that person when you are lonely but to have the courage to visit a friend or go for a bike ride instead of picking up that phone. When you can live through that pain instead of giving in to it, you are growing and maturing. You are taking your first steps toward getting over this relationship and getting on with the rest of your life. In the long run, you are making things better, not worse.

"Is it possible to be friends with an ex?"

Maybe. It depends on the ex.

As I said before, I am friends with several of my ex-boyfriends. I think they are great, and I'm glad they are still in my life. But it didn't happen automatically, and it didn't happen in every case.

No matter what, it is impossible to become "friends" right away. Very few couples can go straight from "We're dating exclusively" to "I'd like to set you up with my friend." There always needs to be a time of healing and readjustment.

It is also impossible to be friends until you have completely talked out the reasons for your breakup, you have forgiven each other for any transgressions, and you are both completely at peace with each other and with the fact that the relationship ended. If one person is still harboring bitterness or resentment toward the other, if there are issues you have to avoid in conversation, or if one person wants to reconcile, a friendship will not work.

If there was sexual activity in the relationship, the odds of being able to build a successful friendship are much slimmer. It is extremely difficult to overlook the bond that resulted from your activity and return to a platonic friendship.

The same is true if the relationship was particularly tumultuous or if one person or the other is extremely immature or emotionally unstable. It requires a great deal of maturity to be able to put the past aside and build a new relationship, and people like this don't generally have what it takes.

How long does it take? Put it this way. You are ready to be friends when this person no longer has any significant emotional power over you. If this person can still make you cry, or if you feel jealous at the thought of this person dating someone else—you are not ready.

Don't be too hard on yourself if you don't wind up friends with all of your ex's. It is a rare relationship that can make the transition successfully. Far more try in an effort to "hang on" to at least part of the relationship, and these end up making themselves miserable in the process.

Old Love / New Love

"What if you have a boyfriend and an old 'love' comes back?"

Uh-oh.

Why is he an "old love"? Why did you break up? Did things not work out? Was he mean or abusive or dishonest or unfaithful? Do you have any reason whatsoever to believe that things are any different now?

It is easy to have warm, wonderful feelings for an "old love". Time tends to erase the bad memories and leave only the happy ones. The memory of your ex may be clouded in vague, happy thoughts. Your current boyfriend, however, is a solid, present reality. He has faults as well as good traits, and I am sure that the faults look a lot bigger compared to Mr. Perfect-Man-from-the-Past.

No one can tell you what to do, especially without knowing the people involved. If you are feeling conflict over this, maybe you need to get away from both long enough to sort it out. That is what being single is all about. But don't throw away a perfectly good "present" over the distorted memories of a "past" that has already failed once.

No Boyfriend/No Love?

"I have felt very lonely (no boyfriend).
I'm seventeen and I'm sick of it.
My self-esteem is very low. What do I do?"

I'm so sorry you feel this way! You should not have to.

If you are lonely, a boyfriend is *not* the way to cure the problem. In fact, I guarantee that it will only make it worse.

Our culture so often links self-esteem to getting attention from the opposite sex and being "in love". This is distorted and downright cruel.

If you are lonely, the best way to deal with your loneliness is by reaching out and making friends. Boyfriends are often temporary. Good friends are permanent—they stick with you through your life, and they don't "break up" with you when they find another friend.

You didn't mention your family. If you have one, spend time with them. Work to build those relationships and to make them strong. They will be your family for life, so you may as well get along as well as possible.

Do things that get you out of yourself. Find out what talents God gave you and develop them. Reach out in love to others who are lonely—people who are sick, people in nursing homes, and so on. It is amazing what giving a little love can do.

Most important of all, of course, is to develop a relationship with the divine Source of all love—God. Your self-esteem should not come from a boyfriend. It should not come from your family or your friends. It should come from the fact that you are created in the image and likeness of God and that He loved you enough to die for you. That love, dignity and respect you will *never* get from a mere mortal boyfriend! Remember what God did for you and how much He loves you. Stay in regular contact with Him.

I know all of this may be easier said than done. If you are feeling bad about yourself, and if it doesn't get better with new friendships and prayer, make a couple of appointments with a good Christian therapist. I honestly believe that good, Christ-based counseling can help *everyone* at one point or another in his life. There are often deeper emotional reasons for our insecurities and fears. Find out what yours are, expose them to the light and then trust God to help you to deal with them.

Until you have done all this, don't worry about finding a boyfriend. Worry about finding yourself. Then, when it is time, you will be in a much better position to pick a *great* guy, instead of just taking the first one to come along.

11

For Teens Only

"How many teens in the U.S. are sexually active?"

It is impossible to answer a question like this exactly. There is no "registry of sexual activity" where people report when they've lost their virginity. If there were, we could just punch up a code in a computer and get a precise number.

But I did run across some information that may surprise you. A recent Roper poll showed that 64 percent of U.S. high-school students are virgins (Roper Starch Worldwide poll, in conjunction with SIECUS [Sex Information and Education Council of the United States], 1994.)

Whenever I discuss this poll in a talk, hands immediately go up. "Really?" "Are you sure?" "Whom did they ask?"

In today's climate, people have a hard time believing that everybody in the world isn't engaging in frequent sexual activity. After all, if you watch TV or go to movies, it's easy to get the impression that *everyone* is having sex on an extremely regular basis. Most people on TV seem to spend their lives falling in and out of love, and sex is what you do as soon as you fall in love, right? Sexual activity seems to be an essential part of life.

People in real life, especially in high school and college, tend to respond to this by making sure people think *they're* sexually active, too—whether they are or not. In a way you can't blame them. Society makes frequent sexual activity seem so "normal", and in a climate like that, no one wants to seem "abnormal".

But the Roper people found something different. For all of that talk, a majority of high-school students are virgins.

The poll also found that, out of the students who had engaged in sexual activity, 54 percent wish they had waited. I found that to be a fascinating statistic. Educators tend to assume that teenagers who have begun sexual activity will always continue to be sexually active. This poll indicates a different attitude. Over half of sexually active teens, roughly one-fifth of all teens, regret engaging in sexual activity.

That finding should make us take a good, long look at our approach to sex education. Here we see that 64 percent of our teenagers aren't sexually active. An additional 20 percent regret becoming sexually active. That's more than 83 percent of high-school students who are obviously open to abstinence, as indicated either by their personal abstinence or by their expression of regret for not abstaining.

Where is this so-called "majority" of teenagers who "are going to do it anyway"? I don't see it. I see a lot of single people of all ages confused about what's expected of them and feeling that they should be "doing it" because everyone else is. I see society feeding that expectation. And I see educational programs responding by assuming that we're all sexually active.

Teenagers, take heart. You're really not alone. There's a

"silent majority" of you out there, living lives of respect for your sexuality despite enormous pressures. So try not to be so silent about it! Find each other and support each other—and let the rest of the world know you're there!

Teen Mothers

"What is so bad about teenaged girls getting pregnant? I for one would like to get pregnant. Just because I'm a teenager doesn't mean I wouldn't make a good mother."

"If children are a gift from God, then why do we get down on teenagers having children?"

One of the most interesting aspects of the current teen pregnancy problem is the fact that more and more teenaged girls are getting pregnant *on purpose.* This is, as we have discussed, a world that offers very little love, leaving many teenagers starved for real, authentic affection and attention. Many girls see a solution in pregnancy. Their baby, they believe, will be someone who will provide the love that is missing in their lives.

Unfortunately, however, babies are more than little love machines. They are drool machines. They are eating machines. They are machines that frequently experience minor and major breakdowns. Babies are very high maintenance.

I am not one of those people who believe that pregnancy is a terrible thing. In fact, I think pregnancy is incredibly beautiful. In pregnancy, we cooperate with God in performing His very favorite act—bringing a new life into the world. Many terrific people have come into the world through pregnancy.

Nor do I believe that the way to stem the teen pregnancy crisis is just to warn teenagers about the absolute horrors of pregnancy and single parenthood. That philosophy is not encouraging them to abstain from sex—it is just leading them into the abortion clinics.

Nevertheless, none of this is to say that pregnancy is *desirable* for an unmarried woman—particularly a teenager. As beautiful as it is to bring a new life into the world, it is also a *huge* responsibility. Babies need to be fed, changed, comforted and taught. Throughout their lives, they require fairly large amounts of money—for diapers, baby food, Cub Scouts, bicycles, prom dresses and four-year colleges.

Most importantly, children need to be molded into healthy, well-adjusted adults. God doesn't give us children just so that we can make them the most popular people in the school. He gives them to us so that we can mold them into followers of Christ and so that we can lead them to live forever with Him in heaven, where they belong. God loves each child more than any parent ever could. But He puts that child in the parent's care. That is a big responsibility, and each parent will have to answer for it in the end.

I am sure many of you know single parents. Perhaps some of you were raised by single parents or are single parents yourselves. You know better than anyone that single parents are often heroes. They work hard, and they often raise very loving, wonderful, well-adjusted children. But any single parent will tell you that he is doing the work of two people.

Teenagers simply are not ready for this kind of responsibility. They still have a great deal of growing and learning to do for themselves, so that they will have more to offer their children when they do become parents. They need to complete their own educations. They need to define their interests and pursue them. They need to date freely and to figure out with whom they are compatible. They need to play a little, while they have the chance.

Teen parenting complicates all of this. Babies cry in the middle of the night, making a good night's sleep almost impossible. Babies require twenty-four-hour-a-day attention, making it difficult to do much of anything else. Want to go to school? You'll need to arrange for (and pay for) day care. Want to go to a party? You'll have to get a baby-sitter. Want to do your homework? If the baby is crying, homework will have to wait.

Babies also need something else: two role models. God created us with very complex psycho-sexual developmental needs, and those needs are best met by having both male and female role models. Children really do want to have a father and a mother. When it doesn't work out that way, for whatever reason, the children suffer. Sometimes tragedy strikes—a parent is killed or severely injured, a woman become pregnant because of rape, a parent walks out on the family. These are difficult situations, and many people respond heroically. But to get pregnant deliberately, knowing that the child is not being brought into a committed marital relationship, is to bring a child into the world at a severe disadvantage. It is selfish and irresponsible. It is not a good idea.

"Going to 'Do It' Anyway"

**"Teenagers are going to 'do it' anyway.
Shouldn't they at least have protection?"**

There's a prevalent attitude in society that people, especially teenagers, are "going to 'do it' anyway". Oddly enough, I don't often hear this phrase from teenagers who insist *they* are going to do it anyway. I generally hear it from adults, or from teenagers who are abstaining themselves but have heard adults say that *other* teenagers are going to do it anyway.

I don't buy it. *Cattle* are going to do it anyway. I don't give many talks to cattle. *Now, when you go on your little cow dates, be sure to stay out here in the pasture. Don't go back there into the woods—you may get into trouble.*

Dogs in heat are going to do it anyway. But people don't go into heat. People are not animals. We have brains and free wills, and we are capable of determining what is good for us and what is bad for us and choosing accordingly, even if our drives are trying to push us in a different direction.

For the record, I don't believe that teenagers are any exception to this rule. Unfortunately, the educational establishment often doesn't seem to share my confidence.

In fact, I frequently find among "adults" a very irritating habit of copping out on teenagers.

What impact does it have on a teenager to say, "You should abstain, but if you can't or don't, be sure to use a condom"? What is the expectation here? That it is not possible to abstain? That abstinence is optional?

A friend of mine once pointed out, "When my husband goes on a business trip, I expect him to be faithful. I don't say, 'Honey, try not to cheat on me, but in case you do, I left some condoms in your briefcase.'" There is no room for double messages when the stakes are high.

I believe that teenagers are capable of much more than "adults" give them credit for. I have found that when we let them know we believe in them, they're capable of truly great things.

"Too Young"

"What about the student who meets Mr. Right at age sixteen. Suppose they are certain of their love for each other and are planning to marry. How do you argue for chastity when a ten-year wait is necessary?"

"What if you've met the person you're going to marry, but you are too young now. Would sex be wrong if both of you have promised to stay with each other?"

"Too young" is the key phrase here. Why can't you get married? Because you are too young. Why are you too young?

The years between the ages of sixteen and twenty-one or so are crucially important. We do more changing, growing and developing in those years than we will probably do for the rest of our lives. It is safe to say that most of us are very different people at twenty-one from what we were at sixteen.

So perhaps two sixteen-year-olds are really in love. Perhaps they want to get married. I am not questioning that they can be in love. But the reason they can't get married *now* is that they are still growing and changing. They still have a lot to do. They need to chase their goals and change their majors and finish school and decide what they want to be when they grow up. They need to see if their love can survive all those changes.

Sex is about giving yourself totally and completely to another person. But before you can give yourself, you need to *become* yourself—your adult self.

Sex doesn't say, "I love you right now and I hope we'll stay together." It means, "I have sacramentally united myself to you, and I give myself completely to you." You can't do that until you have a complete "self" to give.

Teens in Love?

"Do you think teenagers can be in love?"

Yes. All teenage relationships are not tortured stories of infatuation and pain. I believe that many young couples can be very deeply in love.

The test of that love is in what they do about it. Do they look out for what is best for each other? Do they allow each other enough space to do all of the changing and growing that the teenage years require, even if that means risking losing the relationship? Do they encourage other friendships? Do they resist the temptation to monopolize each others' time? Do they allow each other to pursue their goals, even if it means going to different schools or living in different states? Do they allow each other the freedom to leave the relationship if one should change or "outgrow" the other during this crucial time? Do they have the patience to postpone marriage until they are mature, competent adults, ready to build a family together?

Most importantly, do they respect each other sexually? Do they look out for what is best for each other, even if it means denying a very strong physical urge? Can they put their long-term happiness ahead of their short-term sexual drives?

This is a pretty tall order, but I think there are young couples out there who are up to it. And I say, "More power to them."

Interest in Sex

"Why are girls not as interested in sex as guys are?"

It is always impossible to speak in broad generalities like this. There are a lot of men who, although they certainly would enjoy sex on a physical level, are much more interested in developing a relationship on the emotional and spiritual level. At the same time, there are women who seem to be after "just one thing". It is true, however, that there are certain differences between men and women in their sexual "wiring".

The first difference, as we just discussed, is the fact that males reach their sexual peak earlier than females. This means that, for the most part, teenaged boys tend to be more interested in sex, or more easily sexually aroused, than teenaged girls.

Psychologists say that it is perfectly normal for teenaged girls not to be particularly interested in sexual intercourse at all. There are differences of course—no two women are exactly the same. Some young women *are* interested in intercourse. Some teenaged women marry and have healthy marital sexual relationships. But I have spoken to many, many teenaged women who are worried about themselves, either because they don't want to have intercourse or because they have done it and have not enjoyed it. They are afraid, in this sex-saturated world, that something is wrong with them and that they are missing out on the greatest experience they could ever have. Let me repeat: *It is perfectly normal for teenaged women not to be interested in sexual intercourse.* They are still far from reaching their sexual peak. Most girls who are uninterested in sex as teenagers find that, as they move into their twenties, their attraction to the idea of sexual intercourse grows, and they find living chastity to be a little bit more difficult.

A second reason women at times tend to be less interested in sex is because the sex/relationship connection seems to be stronger in females than males. Males, whether they like it or not, can be sexually aroused by seeing someone on the street, someone they may not even know. Female sexual arousal is generally more tied to the relationship itself. Women's sexual attraction is often based on their feelings of love, intimacy or attachment to a specific person. That makes women less sexually "interested" in males in general but more interested in men with whom they are in love or with whom they share an emotional attachment.

Teen Dating?

"You said dating is about finding someone to marry. Teenagers aren't ready to get married. What is the purpose of dating for us?"

When you are younger, you are not usually thinking about marriage. You are just trying to figure out the opposite sex in general—and that is a difficult job. (Why do girls cry even when there is nothing wrong? Why do guys not *know* how they are feeling?) It is important, however, to try to understand the opposite sex, because without doing so, you will never figure out which one of them you want to marry.

This is why, when you are younger, it doesn't make much sense to have one-on-one dating. You are nowhere *near* ready to think about marriage, and there is no real reason to "commit" yourself artificially to one person. Group "dating" is a much better idea. You should have big groups of friends of both sexes and spend time together as a group, so that you can get to know a *lot* of members of the opposite sex in an informal, low-pressure way.

"What is a good age to start dating?"

There is no reason to rush into dating. As I just said, dating is about finding a marriage partner. It can put a lot of pressure on your life, and there is no reason to deal with that pressure if you are not ready for it.

I don't think there is one particular age when a person is somehow magically "ready" to start dating. Different people mature at different rates.

I believe that someone is ready to start dating when he is mature enough to do two things. First, this person needs to be able to put dating into its proper place in his life, without allowing it to interfere with other important activities like schoolwork and family. And second, he needs to be able to say "no" to sexual advances, firmly and confidently. If you can't do those two things, dating is guaranteed to make your life worse, not better. And who needs that?

"Do you think it is right to have a relationship with a big age gap?"

I am asked this question frequently, usually in the context of an older guy dating a younger teenaged girl.

A big age gap can be dangerous for a couple of reasons. One, until a woman reaches her early twenties, she is still changing and growing emotionally. This is a very important process, and it requires going through certain steps. It also requires being around other people who are at roughly the same level of maturity she is. Spending time with someone who is much older, and who has already gone through those steps, can cause her to skip them altogether and to miss out on important developmental growth.

I can already hear a lot of you saying, "But I'm so much more mature than all of these morons at the high school! I'd much rather be around him than around all of these 'children'." Just about everyone has felt that way at some point. It's normal. But it doesn't mean you are quite as mature as you think. People mature in different ways at different rates. You may be more mature than your high-school friends in *one* way, but that doesn't mean that you are, across the board, ready to skip out on an entire phase of your development.

There is also the question of this older person. Who is he? And why is *he*, a supposedly mature adult, picking up dates at the local high school? Why is he not dating women closer to his own age? Often the issue is not so much that *you* are so very mature as it is that *he* is immature. An immature twenty-five or thirty-year-old is far more hopeless than an immature eighteen-year-old. It is too late for him to go back to high school (although, through you, he may be trying). It is not too late, however, for you to go through all of the steps and do it right the first time.

It is also likely, although not a foregone conclusion, that this older man is more sexually experienced than you are or a guy your own age would be. It is definitely true that it is more difficult to say "no" to someone older and more intimidating to you.

These are some of the dangers of high-school girls dating much older guys. I know they may seem like generalizations, but do listen carefully. "Love" is often blind, especially when it is combined with the ego boost you get from receiving attention from an "older" man. But don't be swept off your feet. Older men who date much younger women often are not the bargain they seem to be.

"Is it healthy to have one boyfriend for all of high school?"

"Do you think long-term relationships in high school are good?"

For the most part, I don't think long-term high-school relationships are a very good idea.

As I said earlier, I do believe there are exceptions. Some people have very healthy high-school relationships. Some people do go on to marry their high-school sweethearts and live happily ever after. I have seen it happen. Many others, however, marry their high-school "sweethearts" when they are too young to make a good decision, and the marriages fail miserably. Far, far more just stick around in a relationship that is, in many ways, making them miserable and end up missing out on much of what is good about the high-school years.

The whole idea of "long-term" relationships has, in my opinion, gotten totally out of hand. All over the country, I talk to young men and women in the middle of important developmental years who are saddled in these fake "marriages" that restrict them, monopolize their time, and offer them no security besides "I promise not to date anyone else until I dump you." These arrangements usually make these people upset far more often than they make them happy. Ironically, most of these relationships end in a breakup, which upsets the people involved all the more.

What kind of system is this?

Why do people get involved in relationships like this? Often, they are looking for love. They are lonely. They want to find someone who will be "there" for them all of the time. A girl thinks, "If only I had a boyfriend, everything would be wonderful." She then gets a date, maybe with someone she likes very much, but things aren't so wonderful. This should come as no surprise. He is expecting a cheeseburger and a movie. She is expecting him to stick around and meet all her emotional needs. There is a little more pressure on him than he expected.

With the widespread breakdown of the family, many single people, especially teenagers, are trying to turn to boyfriends and girlfriends to fill the gap. It doesn't work. The dating relationship is, by definition, temporary. Dating is about finding out if you are compatible with someone and dumping him if you are not. If, however, you are dependent on this person for love, it won't be so easy to get out when you need to. Additionally, if you are too needy while you are with the person, the resulting pressure will probably cause more tension than the relationship can withstand.

Long-term relationships also pose a danger to chastity. Ask anyone who has ever been in this kind of relationship: The longer two people are together, the more difficult it becomes to resist sexual temptation. This is true whether these two people are deeply in love or just trying to use each other to bring some kind of love into their lives.

It all boils down to this: You are ready for an exclusive,

not-dating-anyone-else relationship when you are ready seriously to explore the idea of spending the rest of your life with this particular person. Why else would you tie yourself down to someone? If you don't plan to explore the idea of marriage, then you are just guaranteed to have to break up with this person sooner or later. Why set yourself up for that kind of pain?

In order to reach the point of being ready to commit to a relationship, you have to have your own life in order. You have to possess a certain level of maturity and emotional stability. You have to be choosing this person *freely*, not out of any emptiness or neediness. You have to be, to a certain extent, a *whole* person, healthy and ready to give.

As I said, this can happen in high school, but I think it is the exception rather than the rule. The signs of a *good* high-school relationship are that the relationship makes you a better person. Your grades should go up, not down. This relationship should make you laugh more and smile more, not cry more. Your relationships with your family and friends should improve, not deteriorate. You should feel free to go where you want to go and do what you need to, without feeling tied to this person.

There is no need in the world to rush all of this. Don't get sucked into the high-school mentality of *having* to have a boyfriend or girlfriend. Concentrate on *yourself*, on growing in your skills and abilities, in your maturity, and in your relationships with God, your family and your friends. Then you can skip being trapped in a painful, traumatic, dead-end high-school relationship and can wait until you are ready to explore something more permanent.

"Do you think it is important to find a Christian boyfriend when you are only a teenager?"

I don't think it is particularly important to find a steady boyfriend at *all* when you are a teenager. As we discussed in the last question, however, the time to "commit" to a boyfriend is when you are ready to start exploring the possibility of marriage with someone. At that point, you should definitely be looking at a Christian.

Think about it. This is the person with whom you may spend the rest of your life. This person will help you raise your children. As we have discussed before, if you don't hold the same beliefs about what life is about, you are going to have some serious problems. It would be difficult to raise believing children when Daddy doesn't even believe.

If you want to meet non-Christian guys, fine. If you want to go out for coffee with them, go for it. If you want to tell them about your faith, more power to you. But don't get seriously involved with a non-Christian figuring that you can "convert" or "change" him. Remember, marriage is a "come as you are" party. Don't get romantically involved until *after* the conversion.

Parents

"Does introducing your boyfriend to your parents scare him away or seem too serious?"

It shouldn't. Parents have good reason to want to meet a guy you are dating. (See the Mr. Senior-with-a-Van story in Chapter 8.) A mature guy, the kind of guy you want to be dating, should understand that. I would think he would *want* to meet your parents, to learn more about you and what your family is like.

If a guy resists meeting your parents or won't come into their house to pick you up for a date, consider this a red flag. He is not a "grown-up" yet.

"If parents went through the same thing, why can't they relate?"

Parents were once teenagers. Then they grew up and had a child whom they love dearly and want to protect from all of the dangers in the world. They are well aware of those dangers, and they tend to remember the dangers better than they remember other aspects of being a teen—like the incredibly intense emotions you are feeling.

You, on the other hand, are somewhat new at this teen thing. You are well aware of the intense emotions that go with being a teen, but you are largely oblivious to the dangers that lurk all around you. Sure, you have been told about them, and you are vaguely aware that bad things can happen, but you are fairly sure they won't happen to *you*.

So the trick is to talk and to listen. You need to listen to your parents, because they have a perspective you don't. They have been all the way through things you have only been halfway through. They often know what they are talking about.

And you need to talk to your parents *honestly*. You need to remind them of the confusion and the intensity of teenage feelings. You need to reassure them that you are acting maturely (and then act maturely!). You need to share with them whatever plans you may have made to save sex for marriage or to take an honors class or go to college or to do volunteer work. If you are really becoming so mature and trustworthy, show them! It'll be a lot easier for them to trust you if you give them good reason.

And don't be ashamed to ask for their help and guidance. After all, you are not expected to know it all just yet. In the meantime, a little communication goes a long way.

"Do you think people who have premarital sex have a harder time with their parents?"

Definitely. I have never seen a teenager's relationship with his parents *improve* as a result of premarital sex, that's for sure.

There is a reason for this. You have to keep secrets from them. You are doing something that could hurt you, and if they found out about it, they would probably be worried and hurt and upset—with good reason.

Improved parental relationships is only one of many reasons it is smarter to live chastity.

"Do you feel that teenagers who have overprotective parents will be more likely to be rebellious?"

Statistics show that to be true. But what a teenager considers overprotective and what an objective outsider would call overprotective are often two very different things.

When I was in high school, I considered any restriction my parents placed on me (there really weren't that many) to be "overprotective". I was bright and smart and mature, of course, and I did not need them telling me what to do. Of course, when I went too far and got into trouble, I always went running to them to bail me out.

I realized how lucky I was one day when I was complaining to a friend about how strict my parents were. He said, "At least they care." He told me about a time he had been snowbound in the mountains for three days, unable to reach his father. When he finally got through on the third day, his father hadn't noticed he was gone.

Protective parents aren't always so bad.

"What do you do when your ex wants you back, but your parents totally hate him?"

If your parents totally hate him, you may want to listen to what they have to say.

Love, as we discussed, is blind. It is easy to get caught up in how he makes you feel, or how funny or sensitive he is, and you think they just don't know him like you do. True, your parents may not see his funny side or his sensitive side. But bear in mind, they may be seeing his "snotty, arrogant side" or his "potential to commit a major felony side", which you, in your bliss, are missing.

Talk to them. Ask them what their objections are. Take those objections seriously. Think about what they are saying. Ask others what *they* think of him. Remember that one of the signs of true love is that friends and family approve. If several people disapprove, you may be missing something.

Ask yourself this: Is he *really* good for you? When you are missing him and wanting him to hold you again, it is easy to forget all the times he made you cry. Your parents, on the other hand, haven't forgotten. They love you and they want what is best for you.

In the end, if you live in your parents' house, respect their wishes. You don't have to (and you should not) deny your feelings for this person, but try to understand them. If the relationship wasn't healthy, try to deal with the feelings in a positive way. If you believe he is good and mature and wonderful, remain friends. If it is meant to be, when you are old enough and out on your own, he will still be there.

"My friend wants to go out with this guy, but she has never really discussed dating with her parents. Normally I wouldn't condone this dating, but this guy is really nice. How should she approach this subject with her parents?"

Respectfully and honestly. She should ask them their views on the subject. She should explain to them that she has met a very nice guy. She should listen to any concerns they have and tell them how she plans to address them. If she has made a commitment to save sex for marriage, she should share it with her parents, as well as the steps she is taking to insure chastity in dating. She should allow them to meet him and agree to abide by all of their rules for curfew, and so on.

And in the end, again, she should abide by their decision. If he is a nice guy and genuinely interested in her, he will understand, and he will still stick around and be her friend.

The Media

"What effect does the promotion of sex through the media have on teenagers?"

A very bad one. If you watch much TV or go to many movies or listen to much popular music, you get the impression that everyone in the world is having sex on a very regular basis. Sometimes they even expect you to watch.

These kinds of attitudes can have an impact on anyone, but especially teenagers who are figuring out the world for the first time.

There are several things you can do about this. First of all, watch what you put into your brain. The phrase "garbage in, garbage out" is true. If you want to live chastity, you should not allow sexual lies and misinformation into your head. This is especially true when it comes to explicit sex scenes. Sexual images, as I have said, are very powerful. They stay in your brain, and they flash back at the least opportune moments—like when you are trying to be chaste.

Don't go to a movie if you know there will be an explicit sex scene. And if a scene like that shows up in a movie that you didn't expect to have one, don't watch. Go get popcorn. Go to the rest room. Talk to your date. ("Look at me for now. I don't want those images in my brain, and I sure don't want them in yours.")

Listen to your music. If the lyrics are sexually offensive, stop playing the song. Garbage in, garbage out. You don't need those lyrics in your brain.

Boycott products. If you see sexually offensive advertising aimed at you, don't buy what they are selling. Companies use advertising like that because they think it works. Don't let it work on you.

Don't just passively accept the media's messages. Question them. Challenge them. Don't let them pigeonhole you, and don't let them manipulate you.

Peer Pressure

"How do I avoid peer pressure?"

Work to build a group of friends who accept and support what you believe in. It will be difficult to be strong without a support group like that. If you don't have friends who will support you, go to a church youth group or prolife group and try to find people who would be supportive friends. They don't have to be your only friends, but they will be the ones who will help you when things get rough.

Epilogue

Chastity is not just the answer to the question: "How do I avoid AIDS, or pregnancy, or STDs?" Chastity also helps us to answer the deeper questions: "Who am I?" "Who is God in my life?" "How do I find love?"

Whether you are a college student, a single adult or a teenager, I hope that some of what you have found in these pages applies to your own life. And I pray that, as a result of what you have read here, you have made a commitment, or a recommitment, to living a life of real love—chastity.

We talked in the beginning of the book about how the Church doesn't *make* us do anything. We have free will, and our free decisions determine the course of our lives. But make no mistake. Making a commitment to living chastity is not optional for the Christian. Deciding to respect our sexuality is a part of the decision to follow Jesus Christ. Christ never said, "Some of My followers keep My commandments, and some of My followers don't." He said, "If you love Me, keep My commandments."

He knew we would stumble and fall sometimes. He knew He was asking us to follow a "narrow road". He expects us, however, to try. When we fall, He expects us to repent, to get back up, to brush ourselves off and to start trying all over again.

Chastity does not come automatically. As a result of original sin, we are inclined to do things we should not do.

Our hearts are not totally corrupt, but neither are they completely pure. As John Paul II says, the human heart is a "battlefield" between love and lust. Each is constantly trying to gain the upper hand.

The strength to live chastity does not, repeat, *does not* come from us. It is a gift from God—a gift available to anyone who asks it of Him. Anyone who commits to a life of chastity but doesn't pray for the strength to live it is setting himself up for failure.

Chastity *does* get easier over time. It is, as I said before, like a muscle. When you first start lifting weights, it seems very, very difficult. But as you continue to work out, over weeks and months, the same amount of weight becomes easier to lift. The load is still just as heavy, but you have developed the muscle you need to handle it. And prayer is like having the Holy Spirit behind you with His finger under the barbell, helping you to lift.

Likewise, every time you encounter a tempting situation, call on the Holy Spirit and successfully resist, you become a little bit stronger, a little more chaste. You develop a little bit more spiritual "muscle".

Please, don't ever take chastity for granted. Don't ever start to think you have developed enough muscle and/or that you no longer need the Holy Spirit behind you, helping you to lift that weight. You do. Without Him, that barbell would come crashing in on your head, no matter how strong you think you are.

Don't ever think you have attained perfect chastity. You have not. I have not. There is no such thing in this life. You are still running around in a human body, and that body is still programmed to respond in certain ways to certain stimuli. It is when you take your guard down, when you stop praying because you think you have it all figured out, that you are in the most danger.

Christ, in speaking to His disciples, said, "You live in My love when you keep My commandments, just as I keep the Father's commandments and live in His love. I tell you this that My joy may be your joy, and that your joy may be complete" (Jn 15:9). That, in a nutshell, is why I do what I do. I don't give these talks just because I want to help you avoid AIDS, unmarried pregnancy and sexually transmitted diseases. It's true, I don't want to see you go through any of those traumas. But I want more for you than just that. I want you to experience *joy*—the authentic love and joy that Christ was talking about, the joy that comes from following all of His commandments and living our lives according to His instruction manual.

You can't find that joy in "safe sex". You probably won't find it in mere "abstinence" practiced out of fear. But you will begin to find that joy and that peace in living lives of real, authentic chastity.

Don't just abstain. Be radical. Be chaste.

APPENDIX 1

Sexually Transmitted Diseases

AIDS

Nature of disease: AIDS (Acquired Immune Deficiency Syndrome) is a viral infection caused by the human immunodeficiency virus (HIV). The virus attacks primarily the immune cells, destroying them and leaving the body unable to fight off infection.

Course of disease: The virus is transmitted through the exchange of HIV-infected body fluids: blood and blood products and semen. Saliva and tears have been found to contain the virus, but their ability to infect is still unknown. Most cases are caused by intimate sexual contact, contaminated I.V. needles or blood transfusions. The advent of mandatory testing at blood banks has drastically reduced the incidence of transfusion-related transmission.

A person may be infected with the HIV virus, or "HIV positive", for years before developing full-blown AIDS—that is, before experiencing the symptoms that result from damage to the immune system. During this asymptomatic ("silent") time of HIV infection, the infected person is con-

301

tagious, even though no symptoms may be present. Most HIV positive persons are expected eventually to develop full-blown AIDS, and AIDS, at this time, is eventually fatal.

Symptoms: Four to eight weeks after HIV infection, a mild mononucleosis like infection generally appears and then disappears. The virus is sometimes detectable by a blood test as early as six weeks after infection, although in rare cases it can take as long as one to three years for the infection to give a positive reading on an HIV test. But a person infected with the HIV virus is contagious from the moment of infection, even if the virus doesn't show up on a blood test.

As the HIV virus begins to attack the immune system, the infected person often develops enlarged lymph nodes. Symptoms such as fever, weight loss, diarrhea, mouth infections and shingles then begin to develop in some patients. As the immune system is destroyed, more major symptoms can develop. "Opportunistic" infections such as pneumocystis (a kind of pneumonia) and an infection which involves the brain, toxoplasmosis, which a normal immune system would easily fight off, invade the body. Some AIDS patients develop malignancies such as non-Hodgkin's lymphoma and Kaposi's sarcoma. Some develop HIV-related dementia as the virus affects the brain.

Prognosis: HIV is now the leading cause of death among men age 25–44 in major metropolitan areas. From 1981 to 1993, 339,250 cases of AIDS were reported to the CDC, and 201,775 (60.3%) AIDS-related deaths were reported.

Chlamydia

Nature of disease: Chlamydia is an infection caused by the *chlamydia trachomatis* organism. The primary site of infection is a woman's cervix, fallopian tubes and ovaries and a man's urethra and epididymis.

Course of disease: The disease is caused only by sexual intercourse with an infected partner.

Left untreated, a chlamydia infection can ascend the uterus, tubes and ovaries, developing into a serious infection of the pelvic structures known as salpingitis, commonly called Pelvic Inflammatory Disease (PID), and perihepatitis.

Men infected with the chlamydia virus can also develop epididymitis, in which the infection spreads from the urethra into the epididymis. A connection has also been discovered in men between chlamydia infection and Reiter's syndrome, a painful systemic illness.

Symptoms: Up to 70 percent of people infected with chlamydia are completely asymptomatic and unaware that they carry the disease. Symptoms that may occur when the organism multiplies include cervical discharge in women, urethral discharge in men, a burning sensation with urination, urgency or frequency of urination, or pain in the lower abdomen. Symptoms that indicate the infection has progressed to salpingitis (PID) include low abdominal pain and fever.

Symptoms associated with chlamydia are indistinguishable from those due to gonorrhea. The two frequently co-exist.

Symptoms of Reiter's syndrome in men include urethral discharge, a burning sensation on urination, irritated eyes and arthritis.

Prognosis and complications: Chlamydia infection in its early stages is easily treated with tetracycline, doxycycline, erythromycin or azythromycin.

Unfortunately, chlamydia infections often do significant damage to the reproductive system before they're cured. A woman with one episode of salpingitis has a 20 percent chance of being left permanently sterile. Women with a history of salpingitis are at a higher risk of tubal (or ectopic) pregnancies. Miscarriages have also been linked to chlamydia infection as well as chronic pelvic pain.

Salpingitis can lead to abscesses that can necessitate the complete removal of the fallopian tubes, uterus and ovaries. These severe pelvic infections can also lead to death.

In men, chlamydia-induced epididymitis can lead to sterility.

Prevalence: Studies report that up to 40 percent of sexually active single women are found to have blood tests showing antibodies to chlamydia, indicating either past or current infection.[1] Cultures for chlamydia are positive in up to 19 percent of women examined in general gynecological clinics but in up to 31 percent in venereal disease treatment centers. Four to 25 percent of all college students

---

[1] Joe McIlhaney, M.D., *Safe Sex* (Grand Rapids, Mich.: Baker House Books, 1992), 102.

are infected with chlamydia. The *chlamydia trachomatis* is the most common sexually transmitted microorganism in the U.S.

Herpes

Nature of disease: Genital herpes is caused by an infectious virus, *herpes simplex virus* (usually Type II). The virus causes painful blisters in and on the sex organs. Direct contact with infected secretions is required for transmission. HSVII virus is usually transmitted by genital secretions: Herpes is also transmitted by oral secretions.

Course of disease: The incubation period for HSV is usually 2–7 days after first exposure. Following primary infection HSV travels along sensory nerve pathways from the skin to the body of the nerve and remains there latent. Recurrent infections are usually due to reactivation of latent HSV. Sometimes the virus remains dormant for years before an outbreak or remains in the body without *ever* causing an outbreak.

Sixty to ninety percent of people with primary HSV will have a recurrence. Subsequent outbreaks can occur as seldom as once a year or as frequently as several times a month. Menstrual periods, stress, intercourse, tight clothes and other factors can trigger an outbreak. But regardless of whether the virus causes an outbreak, it is still contagious. The surrounding skin can "shed" the virus even when no sores are present.

Symptoms: The first breakout of herpes blisters is usually the most severe. Before the blisters develop, there may be local pain, tingling, itching or burning. Blisters form and then break, leaving sores varying from one-eighth inch to over one inch across. Herpes breakouts are sometimes sufficiently painful to require hospitalization. An outbreak of herpes can also cause enlarged lymph nodes in the groin and flulike symptoms in the form of fever and aching muscles. Urethral involvement can lead to urinary infection.

Prognosis and complications: Herpes is incurable. Once infected with the herpes virus, it remains in the system forever.

Outbreaks of herpes blisters can be treated with acyclovir ointment. The ointment will alleviate pain and help the blisters to clear up more quickly.

For those with frequent outbreaks, acyclovir capsules can be taken orally. Usage is approved only for one-year periods. During that time, outbreaks can be controlled, and 40–75 percent of sufferers will have few outbreaks or none at all.

Herpes can complicate childbirth. Herpes has been associated with increased risk of miscarriage, premature delivery and low birthrate. If the mother is untreated, there is a serious risk of the baby dying. Some babies may acquire HSV in utero leading to congenital infection, bleeding, small brains or seizures.

Prevalence: The *Journal of the American Medical Association* (April 4, 1986) reports a study suggesting that 20 to 60 percent of our total population has genital herpes and that the average American male has almost a 50 percent chance of being infected with the virus. Dr. Mary Guinan of the Centers for Disease Control has said that 23 percent of adult Americans are infected with the virus, but only 25 percent of those have any symptoms. Dr. Joe McIlhaney reports the number for sexually active singles to be 30–40 percent.

Gonorrhea

Nature of disease: Gonorrhea is a bacterial infection caused by the *gonococcus* transmitted almost exclusively through sexual intercourse. Gonorrhea is highly contagious—one encounter with an infected individual brings a 20 percent chance of infection for a man, probably higher for a woman.

Course of disease: When a man contracts gonorrhea he may remain symptomless for a long period of time. During that time, however, he is infected and he can transmit the infection to someone else through intercourse. When symptoms do occur they include a burning sensation during urination, a heavy, pus-like discharge, high fever, skin rash and even arthritis.

Infection in a woman may involve only the vulva, urethra, bladder, vagina and cervix, or it may extend to the fallopian tubes, uterus and ovaries (salpingitis, known as Pelvic Inflammatory Disease, PID). Sometimes the Bartholin's glands in the vulva become infected, causing swelling, abscess and cysts. Surgery is required at this point. If PID develops, it can close a woman's tubes and/or cause the pelvic organs to stick together. Abscesses can develop in the reproductive system. The disease can also involve the rectum or mouth upon genital contact with an infected person.

Symptoms: It is estimated that 80 percent of those infected with gonorrhea are unaware of it in the early stages. Most people develop symptoms within 10 days of exposure. When symptoms do occur, they include a burning sensation with urination and discharge of pus from the urethra. Women may also experience a vaginal discharge or severe pelvic pain in the case of gonorrhea-induced PID. Symptoms include skin rash, high fever or arthritis.

Prognosis and complications: Most uncomplicated gonorrhea generally responds to treatment with antibiotics. However, a strain of gonorrhea has been discovered that is resistant to penicillin. Some of these strains respond to a drug called ceftriaxone, while others resist even this.

When a gonorrhea infection has affected the fallopian tubes, irreversible sterility may have already occurred by the time antibiotics are administered. If PID has developed, much more intensive antibiotic treatment, and sometimes hospitalization, is necessary. PID-related scarring may cause chronic pelvic pain even after the infection is gone and may necessitate partial or total hysterectomy. An infected Bartholin's gland may likewise require surgery and may continue to recur for years. Gonorrhea-related damage to the fallopian tubes significantly raises the risk of tubal pregnancy.

Prevalence: The incidence of gonorrhea is increasing in the United States. Each year, over a million new cases are diagnosed. Gonorrhea- and chlamydia-related PID is the major cause of hospitalization for reproductive-age women.

Syphilis

Nature of disease: Syphilis is an infection caused by the organism *Treponema pallidum.* The organism dies quickly outside of a warm, moist environment and is transmitted primarily by genital contact.

Course of disease: The organism is transmitted via moist tissues of the infected person. Ten to ninety days after initial contact, a chancre, or small sore, will develop at the point of infection—the vulva, vagina, penis, mouth or wherever the disease entered the body. The chancre then usually grows into a small knot, one-half inch to one inch across. The chancre and the resulting knot are painless and often ignored.

In untreated patients, a secondary stage of syphilis can develop six weeks to six months after initial infection. Symptoms include characteristic rashes, malaise, fever, and sore throat. In secondary syphilis the organism spreads throughout the body. In this stage the disease is most contagious. This second stage will pass, even without treatment. A latency period follows, lasting anywhere from several months to twenty years. During this period symptoms disappear and the disease, while doing tremendous damage inside the body, is relatively noncontagious.

When this latent period ends, the serious damage of syphilis becomes apparent. It causes aneurysms of the cardiovascular system, deterioration of the central nervous system and peripheral nerves and damage to bones.

Symptoms: The primary symptom of early syphilis is a small, painless chancre or a slightly larger, but still painless, knot in the mouth or on the genitals. In the second stage, symptoms include headache, skin rash, low-grade fever, fatigue, enlarged lymph nodes and raised growths on the skin.

Prognosis and complications: Syphilis is treated with penicillin, which is generally 100 percent effective in killing the bacteria. The danger is in misdiagnosing syphilis or in failing to recognize it before the latency stage, when it begins to do permanent damage. During latency, large abscesses are formed and entire organs can be destroyed. A patient may sustain irreversible damage to the bones, liver cells, heart valves, blood vessels and central nervous system. Syphilis can cause insanity, paralysis, fatal damage to blood vessels and severe bone deterioration.

Babies of syphilitic mothers can contract congenital syphilis, which can be fatal to the child. Those who do survive are often born with such abnormalities as nose obstruction, fractures of the bones, flattening of the bridge of the nose, enlarged liver and spleen and eye or ear damage.

Prevalence: Syphilis is currently at its highest rate since 1950. Approximately 130,000 cases are diagnosed each year. It has been increasing at a rate of 25 percent a year.

Human Papillomavirus (HPV)

Nature of disease: HPV is a sexually transmitted virus that can result in small, soft warts on the reproductive organs. These warts have been associated with abnormal pap smears and with cancers of the reproductive system.

Course of disease: In men, warts develop on the penis, groin area or scrotum. The warts are highly contagious. Roughly 85 percent of women whose regular sex partners have such warts will develop similar warts within eight months. Women's warts can appear in the vagina, on the cervix, in the groin or on the vulva. The virus can cause changes of cervical or vulvar cells that may develop into precancerous growths. If left untreated, these can eventually change into invasive cervical or vulvar cancer.

Symptoms: HPV can cause soft warts on the genitals. Many, however, who are infected with HPV remain symptomless. Changes to the skin cells and the following precancerous changes can nonetheless take place. Even when warts do occur, they are often so small and painless as not to be noticed, or to be noticed but disregarded. Sometimes women infected with HPV experience vulvar itching, irritation, burning and pain.

Prognosis and complications: HPV warts themselves are usually removed, using acid, freezing, laser or cutting. If this is unsuccessful, injections with interferon are used.

If HPV has led to precancerous or cancerous growths, treatment is more complicated. If an abnormal Pap smear indicated precancerous cells, the cervix is usually either frozen or treated with laser therapy, or minor surgery is performed. If the growth has gone beyond the precancerous stages into full-blown cancer, it must be treated aggressively, with radiation or with radical surgery removing the afflicted area. If vulvar cancer is extensive, the entire vulvar area must be removed. HPV-related cancers kill eight thousand women a year.

In men, the primary risk of HPV is penile cancer. When this type of cancer occurs, it is almost always the result of an HPV infection.

Prevalence: HPV is reaching epidemic proportions in this country. Every year 1.5 million new cases are diagnosed. Up to 46 percent of sexually active singles are infected.

APPENDIX 2

Resources and Telephone Numbers

Crisis Pregnancy

Bethany Ministries: 1–800–BETHANY (1–800–238–4269)

Birthright: 1–800–848–LOVE (1–800–848–5683)

Catholic Charities: 1–800–CARE–002 (1–800–227–3002)

The Nurturing Network: 1–800–TNN–4MOM (1–800–866–4666)

Adoption

Bethany Ministries: 1–800–BETHANY (1–800–238–4269)

Catholic Charities: 1–800–CARE–002 (1–800–227–3002)

Counseling

Human Sciences International: 1–301–365–5347

Post-Abortion Counseling

Project Rachel: 1–800–5–WE CARE (1–800–593–2273)

Homosexuality

Courage: 1–212–421–1426

Other Information

For further information on chastity programs, natural family planning or other issues discussed in this book, contact:

MARY BETH BONACCI

1520 W. Warner Rd.,
Suite 106–138
Gilbert, AZ 85233
(602) 812–1194

Bibliography

General Abstinence/Chastity

*Bonacci, Mary Beth. *Sex and Love: What's a Teenager to Do.* (video) Worcester, Penn.: Vision Video, 1995.

*Groeschel, Benedict. *The Courage to Be Chaste.* New York: Paulist Press, 1985.

*Hillerstrom, P. Roger. *Intimate Deception.* Portland, Ore.: Multnomah, 1989.

McIlhaney, Joe S. *Safe Sex.* Grand Rapids: Baker House Books, 1991.

McDowell, Josh. *Why Wait?* San Bernardino: Here's Life Publishers, 1987.

*Trobisch, Walter. *I Loved a Girl.* San Francisco: Harper-Collins, 1989.

————. *Love is a Feeling to Be Learned.* Downer's Grove, Ill.: Intervarsity Press, 1971.

Asterisks denote my personal all-time favorites.

Theology and Sexuality

Burke, Cormac. *Covenanted Happiness.* San Francisco: Ignatius Press, 1990.

Hogan and LeVoir. *Covenant of Love.* San Francisco: Ignatius Press, 1992.

*John Paul II. *Love and Responsibility.* San Francisco: Ignatius Press, 1993.

May, William. *Catholic Sexual Ethics.* Huntington, Ind.: Our Sunday Visitor, 1996.

Quay, Paul. *The Christian Meaning of Human Sexuality.* San Francisco: Ignatius Press, 1985.

* Smith, Janet E. *Humanae Vitae a Generation Later.* Washington, D.C.: Catholic University of America Press, 1991.

————. *Why Humanae Vitae Was Right: A Reader.* San Francisco, Ignatius Press, 1993.

Homosexuality

Harvey, John. *The Homosexual Person.* San Francisco: Ignatius Press, 1987.

————. *The Truth about Homosexuality: The Cry of the Faithful.* San Francisco: Ignatius Press, 1996.

Schmidt, Thomas. *Straight and Narrow?* Downer's Grove, Ill.: Intervarsity Press, 1995.

Sexual Addiction

Arteburn, Steven. *Addicted to Love*. Ann Arbor, Mich.: Servant Publications, 1991.

Post Abortion

Post Abortion Aftermath. Michael Mannion, ed., Kansas City: Sheed and Ward, 1994.

Natural Family Planning

Kippley, John and Sheila. *The Art of Natural Family Planning*. Cincinnati: CCL, 1982.

Shivanandan, Mary. *Challenge to Love*. Bethesda, Md.: KM Associates, 1988.

Classroom Curricula and Commentaries

Mast, Coleen Kelly. *Sex Respect*. Bradley, Ill.: Respect, Inc., 1990.

————. *Love and Life*. San Francisco: Ignatius Press, 1987.

Richard, Dinah. *Has Sex Education Failed Our Teenagers?* Colorado Springs: Focus on the Family, 1990.